CREATIVE INTERVENTIONS
FOR
TROUBLED CHILDREN & YOUTH

LIANA LOWENSTEIN

Champion Press
Toronto, Canada

Canadian Cataloguing in Publication Data

Lowenstein, Liana, 1965-
    Creative interventions for troubled children & youth

Includes bibliographical references.
ISBN 0-9685199-0-3

    1.Play therapy. 2. Child psychotherapy. 3. Adolescent
psychotherapy. 4. Group psychotherapy. I. Title.

RJ505.P6L68 1999   618.92'891653   C99-900458-1

CREATIVE INTERVENTIONS FOR TROUBLED CHILDREN AND YOUTH

Printed in Canada by Hignell Book Printing.
First Printing, April 1999
Ninth Printing, April 2003

Correspondence regarding this book can be sent to:
Champion Press, c/o Liana Lowenstein, Pharma Plus, PO Box 91012,
2901 Bayview Avenue, Toronto, Ontario, Canada M2K 1H0
Telephone: 416 575 7836 Fax: 416 756 7201
Email: liana@globalserve.net Web: lianalowenstein.com

DEDICATION

This book is dedicated to all those children who have had to face adversity in their lives. Over the years, I have worked with many troubled children and youth, and I am repeatedly amazed at their incredible resiliency. I am often reminded of the following well-known children's song, because like the eensy weensy spider, children have remarkable survival skills, and can overcome adversity:

The eensy weensy spider climbed up the waterspout.
Down came the rain, and washed the spider out.
Out came the sun and dried up all the rain.
And the eensy weensy spider climbed up the spout again.

ACKNOWLEDGMENTS

I am forever grateful to the many children who, during my years of clinical practice, have touched and enlightened me. They are the inspiration that led to the writing of this book.

I would like to thank the many talented colleagues with whom I have had the good fortune to work and who have taught me so much. I would like to express my appreciation to the children, families, staff, and colleagues involved with the Toronto Child Abuse Centre, the Jerome D. Diamond Adolescent Centre, and the SAFE-T Program, who helped foster my professional growth. A very special acknowledgment to Marilynn Lay, a friend, mentor, and gifted clinician, whose life was tragically ended by cancer shortly after we worked together on the publication *Paper Dolls & Paper Airplanes: Therapeutic Exercises For Sexually Traumatized Children.*

My heartfelt thanks to Monty Laskin, John Pearce, and Michael Burns, who so generously donated their time to review my initial manuscript, and who provided me with invaluable feedback on the text and the activities. I am also grateful to Amy Marks, Melissa Collins, Francine Goodman, and Susan Greenbloom, who graciously took the time to carefully read the early drafts, and who provided comments, suggestions, and words of encouragement. Thanks also to Susan Code, who worked quickly and diligently to edit this book.

A sincere thank you to booksellers Patti Kirk and Bill Elleker of Parentbooks, and Mary Derouard of Source Resource, who provided me with advice and encouragement in the area of self-publishing.

I also appreciate the following companies who were kind enough to grant me permission to use their trademarked products in my book: Hasbro Incorporated, YES! Entertainment Corporation, P & M Products Limited, Sony Music and Nestlé Canada.

Finally, I wish to thank my family and friends who offered their support and encouragement during the writing and production of this book.

TABLE OF CONTENTS

ACTIVITIES AT A GLANCE

ACTIVITY	THEME	AGES	MODALITY
Pin the Tail on the Donkey	Assessment	4-10	Group
People in My World	Assessment	4-12	Individual, Group
Butterflies in My Stomach	Assessment	7-12	Individual, Group
Sticky Dots	Assessment	7-16	Individual, Group
Puzzle	Assessment	7-16	Individual, Group
Life's Ups & Downs	Assessment	7-16	Individual
The HOT POTATO Game	Identifying Feelings	4-10	Group, Family
The CANDY LAND Game	Identifying Feelings	6-12	Individual, Group, Family
Finger Paints	Identifying Feelings	4-16	Individual, Group, Family
Basketball	Identifying Feeling	7-16	Individual, Group, Family
Feelings Blow-Out	Identifying Feelings	4-16	Individual, Group, Family
Feelings Tic Tac Toe	Identifying Feelings	7-16	Individual, Group, Family
Stuffed Animals	Coping With Feelings	4-10	Individual
Clay	Coping With Feelings	4-10	Individual, Group, Family
The TROUBLE Game	Coping With Feelings	7-16	Individual, Group
A Lot on My Plate	Coping With Feelings	9-16	Individual, Group, Family
Darts	Coping With Feelings	9-16	Individual, Group
Comfort Kit	Coping With Feelings	12-16	Individual
Magic Carpet Ride	Social Skills	4-7	Group
The YAK BAK	Social Skills	4-12	Individual Group
Hugs	Social Skills	4-12	Group, Family
Building Blocks	Social Skills	7-16	Group, Family
NERDS, RUNTS, and DWEEBS	Social Skills	7-16	Group
Friendship Bracelets	Social Skills	9-16	Group
King or Queen for a Day	Self-esteem	4-10	Group, Family
Smiley Faces	Self-esteem	7-12	Individual, Group, Family
Celebration	Self-esteem	7-16	Group, Family
The PERFECTION Game	Self-esteem	7-16	Individual
Over the Rainbow	Self-esteem	7-16	Individual, Group, Family
The Hero in You	Self-esteem	9-16	Individual, Group, Family

INTRODUCTION

Your nine-year-old client has been a life-long witness to his parents' violent arguments. He is very quiet and guarded in therapy.

Your twelve-year-old client has recently been admitted to residential treatment following her disclosure of sexual abuse by her father. She is withdrawn and suspicious in therapy.

Your six-year-old client is a recent refugee from a war-torn country. She is sullen and pensive in therapy.

Your sixteen-year-old client has just been released from an addiction program within a correctional facility. He is angry and resistant in therapy.

While each of these children and youth seem to struggle with their own unique experiences that contribute to their presentation within the therapy process, they all share one thing in common: they dare you to engage them! Many mental health practitioners have found that an activity-based approach that is appealing and immersed in play is absolutely essential in order for children and youth to embrace therapy. As such, creative techniques that use more than dialogue are proving more effective in getting young people to accept the help they need.

This book presents innovative approaches for working with troubled children and youth. Practitioners need to look beyond resistance and toward creativity if they are to engage children and youth in the counseling process.

ABOUT THIS BOOK

Mental health professionals who provide counseling to children and youth are always seeking new and innovative activities to add to their existing repertoire. *Creative Interventions for Troubled Children and Youth* is a collection of therapeutic activities for use with child and adolescent clients in individual, group or family counseling. I have taken familiar and appealing play activities such as toys, board games, stories and crafts, and transformed them into therapeutic interventions in order to reduce the level of threat and to encourage the acceptance of counseling. The activities serve as tools to help children work through their conflicts and master specific tasks. The structured activities in this book are designed to address a wide range of client populations, including children dealing with family violence, divorce, grief and loss, chronic or terminal illness, substance abuse, anger management, and placement in out-of-home care.

Mental health professionals who provide counseling to children, adolescents, and families, as well as professionals from a number of disciplines, including social work, psychology, child and youth counseling, correctional services, and child psychiatry, will find this book invaluable. The activities can be used in a variety of settings such as children's mental health centers, hospitals, child welfare agencies, youth detention settings, and schools.

Mental health professionals using this book should be well grounded in theory and practice, and have clinical training and a knowledge base in the following areas: child development, psychopathology, child management, art and play therapy, and group counseling. A list of suggested readings is provided at the end of this book for those who wish to broaden their knowledge.

The activities in this book have been divided into five chapters: Assessment, Identifying and Expressing Feelings, Coping with Feelings, Social Skills, and Self-esteem. The book begins with six assessment activities providing clinicians with diagnostic tools to assist in treatment planning. These assessment activities are not intended to form a complete assessment package. Rather, they are exercises that can be integrated into the therapist's existing assessment model.

The remaining four chapters provide activities to help children master key emotional and behavioral competencies. The activities in Chapters Two through Five can be incorporated into counseling sessions to help children and youth identify feeling states, cope with emotional difficulties, strengthen interpersonal skills, and enhance self-esteem. A variety of activities are provided within each chapter, so that practitioners can choose interventions that suit their client's specific needs. The last section of the book describes the graduation ceremony that can be incorporated as part of the child's termination process.

Each activity is described within a framework that recommends age suitability, preferred treatment modality, and appropriate stage of treatment. Materials needed to complete the activity are outlined. (The resource section at the back of the book details where particular materials may be obtained.) Several activities include worksheets that may be reproduced for use with clients. The book includes detailed instructions for all activities and a discussion section that further clarifies application and process.

While detailed descriptions are provided on how to use the activities in this book, the activities can be adapted to suit the distinct treatment needs of each child. Creativity and flexibility are strongly encouraged, so that children are responsive to each intervention, and therapeutic goals are achieved.

Some of the exercises are only appropriate for use in one particular modality, such as individual or group treatment. Other activities are suitable for various modalities, and can be modified. Group exercises can be adapted for use in family and multifamily group sessions. For activities that are being used primarily in an individual or group context (rather than in a family therapy setting), consideration should be given to the manner in which the child's caregivers and larger community will be involved in the child's treatment. However, I believe that effective treatment requires a systemic approach. Therefore, every effort should be made to involve the child's family and community in the child's treatment. Contracting with the child, the child's family, and community agencies can address issues related to client involvement, communication, and confidentiality.

Each activity recommends a suitable client age range. However, some children with developmental delays or learning disabilities may lack the capacity to respond appropriately to a particular activity. If this is the case, the activity may need to be altered to fit the child's developmental capacities.

Although the activities are written using the term "children," many of the activities are appropriate for use with adolescents. The term "children" is used throughout this book, as it was awkward to repeatedly use "children and adolescents."

GUIDELINES FOR THE SELECTION AND USE OF ACTIVITIES

As with the use of any therapeutic intervention, there are several key guidelines that should be considered when selecting and using an activity in a therapeutic context:

Have a strong theoretical foundation

Practitioners should be well grounded in their theoretical orientation before using any activities or techniques in counseling sessions with children. Interventions should not be used indiscriminately in a manner that ignores clinical theory. The activities in this book can be integrated into any theoretical orientation that uses a directive play therapy approach. For example, practitioners who are rooted in the principles of Gestalt and behavior therapy, or psychodynamically oriented play therapy, will find many activities in this book to incorporate into their counseling sessions.

Know your audience

Some children perform below age expectations. This may be due to emotional, behavioral, or cognitive deficits. The child's level of functioning should be assessed before therapeutic interventions are selected. Similarly, the child's capacity for insight, as well as his ability to tolerate emotionally laden material, should be taken into account when developing a treatment plan. The child's interests and abilities should also be considered, to ensure that the selected activity appeals to him, relates to his competencies, and sustains his motivation. If an activity is being used in a group or family context, it should fit the needs and functioning levels of each of the members.

Ensure the activity fits the client's treatment needs

A thorough assessment will form the foundation for the development of a comprehensive treatment plan. Within the treatment plan, goals will be established. The activities selected should fit with the child's treatment goals, and should be used as tools to fulfill these goals. Ultimately, the purpose of treatment is to provide a positive and corrective emotional experience for the child.

Choose activities that fit the stage of treatment

There are three main stages of treatment. In the initial stage, the practitioner engages the child and develops rapport. In the middle stage, the interaction between child and therapist intensifies and the child works on treatment issues. The ending stage is a time to review the child's progress and prepare for the termination of treatment. Activities chosen should be appropriate to the particular stage of treatment, and should be properly sequenced. Beginning engagement interventions should be implemented before activities that are more emotionally intense, or that require the child to take greater emotional risk. Ending activities should consolidate the skills learned during therapy, encourage the child's independence, and celebrate the child's achievements. **Note:** In order to assist the reader in selecting activities that fit the stage of the child's treatment, each treatment activity in Chapters Two through Five indicates the appropriate stage of treatment within which the activity should be used.

Be well prepared in advance of the session

Before using any assessment or treatment exercise, the practitioner should prepare for activity implementation by reviewing the activity, gathering materials, and constructing the activity. The practitioner should consider whether the activity could be implemented in the counseling room available and in the time allotted for the session. Remember children are often unpredictable so the practitioner should plan for various ways the child may respond to the activity. If the practitioner lacks confidence, then practicing and rehearsing the activity with a colleague before the session may be helpful. However, no matter how well prepared the practitioner is for the session, the unforeseen can happen; flexibility is therefore essential.

Keep in mind that all activities have a beginning, middle, and end

When implementing an activity, first consider how it will be introduced to the child. The therapist's enthusiasm, creativity, and overall style will be key factors in determining if the child will become interested and engaged in the activity. As the child moves to a more engaged and ready state, deeper issues can be skillfully explored and processed. When the activity has been completed and sufficiently processed, the therapist provides positive feedback to the child on his completed work, and brings closure to the activity.

In addition to considering how to introduce, process, and bring closure to an activity in a particular session, the practitioner must also be concerned with the impact of the activity on the client beyond the session. Although some activities are designed to bring issues and feelings to the surface, care must be taken to ensure that the child does not leave the session feeling overly stressed or unsupported.

Set firm but fair limits

Lack of boundaries and controls during a treatment activity can overwhelm the child and lead to feelings of heightened anxiety. As such, there is a need to provide the child with limits and structure. The nature and intensity of the limits set will depend on the child's existing capacity for self-control, as well as his responsiveness and ability to handle such limits.

Never force a child to participate in an activity

Coercing a child to participate in a therapeutic activity will increase his level of tension and resistance. It is important to proceed at the child's pace and to engage him in treatment by creating and adapting activities that fit with his interests, abilities, and emotional readiness. If a child is exhibiting strong resistance to a particular activity, respond by exploring his feelings. If, after a thorough exploration of the child's emotional state, the child continues to show resistance, then this may be a cue that the activity is inappropriate for the child. The activity should then be adapted or changed.

When in doubt, focus on the process

Even the most seasoned practitioner can become stuck during a session. When this happens, focus on the process of the session rather than the content of the dialogue or the issues under discussion. In this way, the child can reflect upon the style of interaction and not the particular theme of the activity. For instance, ask the child how he prefers to work within therapy, or how he feels when asked a question. Respond to the child by validating, normalizing, or making a reflective comment.

Listen to the child

Children often feel ignored and unheard. An important role of the therapist is to listen and make the child feel that what he has to say is important. During the activity, focus on the child's verbal and non-verbal cues. Ensure that the focus of the session remains on the child, not the therapist. The therapist should refrain from talking too much, even during silences. The use of reflective listening will not only be helpful to the therapeutic process, but it will also model important listening skills for the child.

Do not underestimate the value of the therapeutic relationship

Regardless of the activity being used, the therapist-client relationship is central to the client's realization of treatment goals. The rapport that develops between therapist and child forms the foundation for therapeutic success. In building a therapeutic alliance, the practitioner must create an atmosphere of safety in which the child is made to feel accepted, understood, and respected. Similarly, the therapist must use sensitivity when processing the child's activities so that he does not feel his work is being judged.

Recognize that the activities are only a part of the client's overall treatment plan

Many children in treatment present with a multitude of problems, and therefore require a comprehensive and multifaceted intervention approach. Individual, group, or family counseling may form part of the child's treatment plan and additional interventions may be needed to address the child's issues. For example, children with very poor self-esteem may benefit from attending a recreational program that reinforces their strengths and talents. Generally, I suggest an interdisciplinary, systemic treatment approach that may involve various modalities of counseling, as well as a combination of other interventions.

Remember that the process is more important than the product

The play-based activities in this book make it is easy for both therapists and children to enjoy the sessions and forget about the process and treatment objectives. Therefore, therapists must remember that these activities are tools for intervening therapeutically with troubled children. By all means create a playful atmosphere, but implement the activities carefully, thoroughly and sensitively, always keeping in mind the child's treatment objectives.

RATIONALE FOR THE USE OF ACTIVITY-BASED TREATMENT

This book is designed for practitioners who use a structured, directive treatment approach. While non-directive play therapy methods have traditionally been utilized to assist children in processing unresolved conflict, directive play therapy provides a concrete approach that facilitates open disclosure and guides children closer to specific treatment issues. Bringing children's issues out into the open in a gentle but direct fashion lets them know that their problems are not shameful, and can be discussed.

The creative and imaginative use of structured activities, games, and exercises is a source of fun, play, and enjoyment for children. Directive activities act as catalysts to capture and sustain the child's interest and motivation, diagnose and assess his issues, and enhance his competency in a variety of areas, including insight, self-expression, interpersonal relationships, communication, and self-esteem.

Within the directive play therapy framework, various techniques are integrated. These include game play, expressive arts, role-playing, music therapy, and storytelling. The activities in this book are designed to appeal to children so that a positive counseling experience results. I hope that these activities serve as an inspiration in creating an engaging therapeutic environment for your clients.

CHAPTER ONE:
ASSESSMENT ACTIVITIES

Each new client presents with unique emotional, cognitive, and behavioral issues. Many children have difficulty verbalizing their presenting issues, because they are reluctant to self-disclose, and they are anxious about the therapeutic process. Activities that are concrete and play-based can be used to engage otherwise resistant children, and can help them express their thoughts and feelings.

The assessment phase is a critical component of the intervention process, as it forms the foundation for effective treatment planning. A thorough and comprehensive assessment should examine key areas, including the child's current life stresses, family and peer relationships, coping skills, available supports, and self-esteem issues. The assessment activities in this chapter can be used as tools to assess these key areas. These activities do not form a complete assessment, but rather, should be incorporated into the practitioner's existing assessment model. Selected activities from this chapter can be combined with additional assessment information, family interviews, collateral reports, and diagnostic measures to evaluate the child and his family, and to formulate appropriate treatment goals.

PIN THE TAIL ON THE DONKEY

Theme: Assessment
Recommended Age Range: 4-10
Treatment Modality: Group

Goals
1. Assess presenting problems and issues
2. Assess interaction with peers
3. Enable verbalization of feelings

Materials
• Pin the Tail on the Donkey Game
• Blindfold
• Tape
• Questions (included)
• Index cards or card stock
• Bag filled with treats, such as candies or stickers

Advance Preparation
Remove any reference to "Happy Birthday" from the Pin the Tail on the Donkey Game. Tape the game to a smooth wall or door at a height that all the children in the group can reach. Copy each question from the list provided onto separate index cards or photocopy the question card sheet onto card stock and cut out each question. **Note:** The questions can be adapted depending on the age of the children and the assessment information to be gathered.

Description
Begin by asking the children if they have ever played Pin the Tail on the Donkey. For those who are unfamiliar with the game, quickly go over the rules and for those who do know it, tell them that the group is going to play a different version, described as follows:

One person is chosen to go first. This player is given a cardboard tail with a piece of tape attached to it (the game should come with these tails.) The leader blindfolds the player, spins the player around twice, and faces the player toward the Donkey Game. The player walks up to the game and sticks the tail onto the picture. The tail must be taped to the first place it touches. If a player misses the tail on the picture, then that player must pick a question card from the stack of index cards and answer the question (the leader can read the question aloud to the group). Once that player answers the question, the other group members have a turn to answer the same question. If the player gets the tail on the donkey, then instead of drawing a question card, that player gets to hand out treats from the treat bag to all the players. The next player then has a turn, and so on, until all the group members have had a turn. The game continues until all of the questions have been answered.

During the game, encourage active discussion among the group members. The leader uses the question cards as a point of departure to help the children talk about their issues and concerns.

Discussion

Since children typically find Pin the Tail on the Donkey enjoyable, they should find this version engaging and relatively non-threatening. During the activity, there is ample opportunity to gather assessment information, observe group dynamics, and enhance peer interaction skills. However, as this activity is immersed in play, it is easy to get caught up in the game, and lose sight of the therapeutic process. The leader, therefore, must play a dual role: encourage the play and at the same time, facilitate the children's verbalizations about salient issues.

Questions
PIN THE TAIL ON THE DONKEY

What's the best thing that ever happened to you?	**What are three things you like about yourself?**
What makes you feel upset?	**What's the best thing about your family?**
What would you like to change about your family?	**What is your biggest worry?**
Tell about a time you felt you did something wrong or bad.	**Tell about a time you cried because you were upset.**
What do you think about a lot?	**If you could make three wishes, what would they be?**

PEOPLE IN MY WORLD

Theme: Assessment
Recommended Age Range: 4-12
Treatment Modality: Individual, Group

Goals
1. Assess family relationships and available support networks
2. Enable verbalization of feelings

Materials
• "People in My World" worksheet (included)
• Four kinds of stickers (i.e. hearts, bees, spiders, teddy bears)
• Paper and a variety of stickers to make a sticker book (optional closing activity)

Advance Preparation
Make sufficient copies of the worksheet.

Description
The therapist introduces the activity by asking the child if he likes stickers (most children will respond with great enthusiasm!) The therapist explains that the child is going to use different kinds of stickers to show how he feels about the important people in his life. The therapist then guides the child through the following exercise:

The first step is to fill in the picture of the world by writing the names of the people who are important to you. Write each person's name in a different section. You may want to include the following people: mother, father, step parent, foster parent, brother, sister, grandparent, aunt, uncle, cousin, therapist, group leader, social worker, counselor, teacher, doctor, police, lawyer, baby sitter, coach, religious leader, friends, or pets.

Next, use the stickers to show how you feel about the people in your world:

Put a <u>heart</u> sticker on the people in your world who you <u>love</u>.

Put a <u>bee</u> sticker on the people in your world who make you <u>angry</u>.

Put a <u>spider</u> sticker on the people in your world who <u>frighten</u> you.

Put a <u>teddy bear</u> sticker on the people in your world who <u>help</u> you.

Note: If this activity is being used with younger clients, modify the above instructions using appropriate language. Begin by explaining the concepts and feelings using examples the children will understand.

As the child is completing the activity, the therapist can ask open ended questions to draw further information from the child, such as, "Can you tell me more about why you put a spider sticker on your dad?" or "I see you put a teddy bear sticker on your aunt to show that she helps you. In what way does she help you?" As a closing activity, the child can make a sticker book to take home.

Discussion

This is a concrete exercise that helps bring the child's feelings and concerns to the surface, so that they may be explored, discussed, and treated. Both comfortable and uncomfortable feelings are included in order to provide balance. During the exercise, the therapist uses supportive and reflective comments to facilitate the child's openness.

This activity is appropriate for the beginning stages of intervention, as it can be used as a tool to assess, identify, and work through the child's issues. Although open communication about thoughts and feelings is encouraged, avoid confrontation. If the child presents as emotionally guarded, this should be noted and addressed later in treatment.

PEOPLE IN MY WORLD

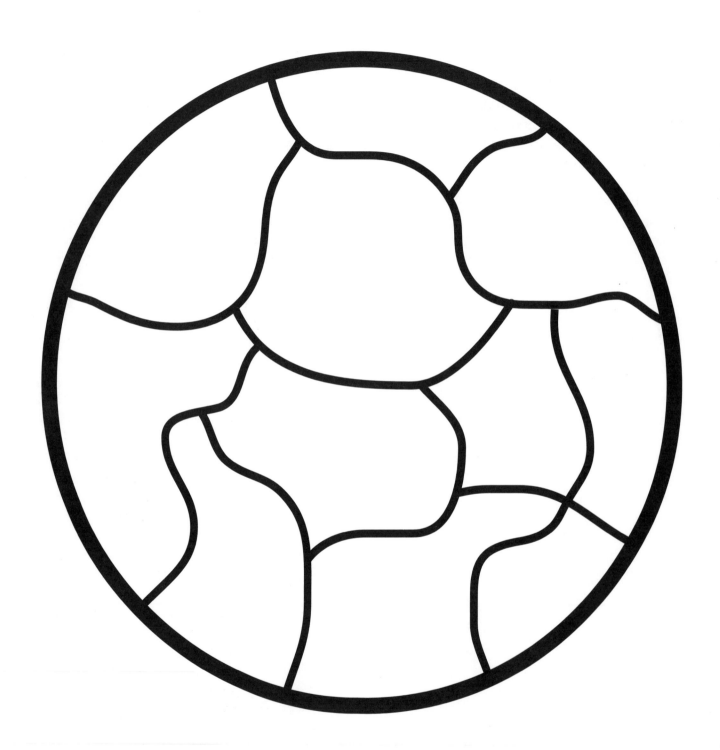

BUTTERFLIES IN MY STOMACH

Theme: Assessment
Recommended Age Range: 7-12
Treatment Modality: Individual, Group

Goals
1. Assess presenting problems and concerns
2. Facilitate awareness regarding how the body reacts to stress
3. Assess and promote problem solving abilities
4. Enable the verbalization of feelings

Materials
• Butterfly outlines (included)
• Scissors
• Glue sticks
• Banner paper

Advance Preparation
Photocopy the sheet with the butterfly outlines, ensuring the child has a number of butterflies of various sizes. Cut out the butterflies.

Description
The therapist introduces the activity by pointing out that everyone has problems and worries. The therapist outlines the different ways the body reacts to stress; for example, when a person is scared, his heart might pound faster, or when a person is sad and about to cry, he might feel like he has a lump in his throat. The therapist then asks the client if he has *ever* heard of the expression, "I have butterflies in my stomach." If the client is unfamiliar with the expression, the therapist can offer an explanation, such as, "When you are worried or nervous about something, your stomach might feel funny or jittery, as if you have butterflies in your stomach. You don't really have butterflies in your stomach, it just feels like you do." Next, spread the banner paper on the floor. The child lies down on it, while the therapist outlines the child's body. Then the therapist gives the child the paper butterfly outlines, on which he writes his worries. Bigger worries are written on the larger butterflies, smaller worries on the smaller ones. The butterflies are then glued onto the child's body outline, inside the stomach. As the child identifies each worry, the therapist can facilitate further discussion by asking open-ended questions, such as, "Tell me more about this worry." The client's problem-solving abilities can be assessed and encouraged by asking, "What could you do about this worry to help yourself feel better?" To assess the client's available support network, the therapist can inquire, "Is there anyone who can help you with this worry?" At the end of the exercise, the child can decorate the body outline.

Discussion
This activity facilitates self-awareness, open communication, problem solving, and catharsis of negative or overwhelming feelings. It is a useful assessment tool that can be applied to a wide

variety of client populations. During the exercise, the therapist can observe and assess the child. The therapist can note whether the child is open and expressive or cautious and avoidant. This is a particularly useful activity with children who have a multitude of presenting problems, as it enables them to communicate to the therapist which problems are most pressing and need priority in treatment. The completed exercise forms a part of the client's assessment, and serves as a blueprint for developing the client's treatment plan.

BUTTERFLY OUTLINES

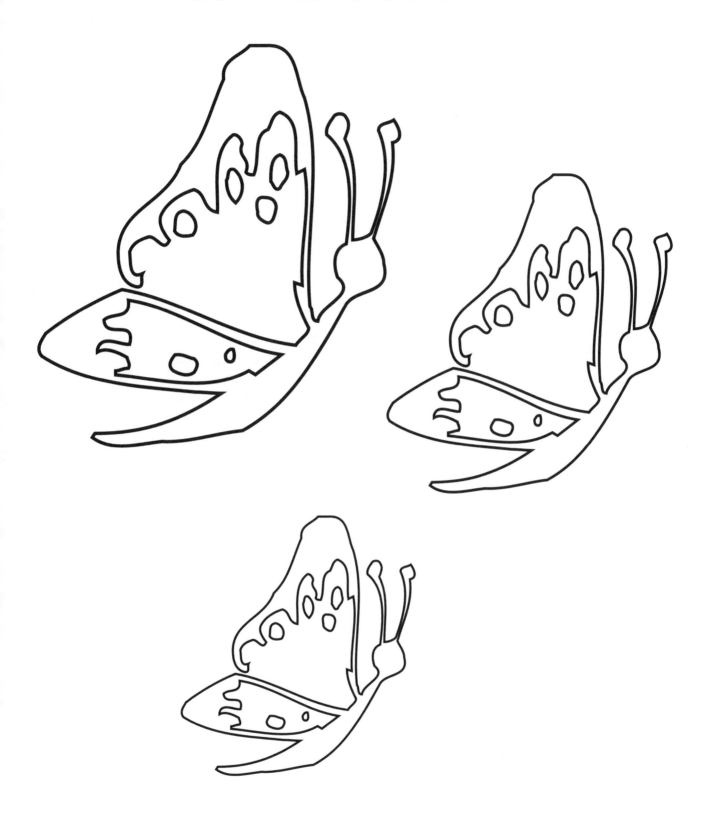

STICKY DOTS

Theme: Assessment
Recommended Age Range: 7-16
Treatment Modality: Individual, Group

Goals
1. Assess current life stresses, symptoms, and coping strategies
2. Enable verbalization of feelings

Materials
• "Survey" worksheet (included) (**Note:** There are two different versions of the survey. The first version is for younger clients, the second is for older clients)
• Small self-adhesive dots

Description
Give the child the worksheet and a sheet of self-adhesive dots. The child reads each statement on the worksheet, and places a self-adhesive dot beside the statements that apply to him. More dots can be placed beside each statement to signify more intense feelings. As the child completes the worksheet, the therapist can generate further discussion about the child's responses.

Discussion
Most children in therapy have problems and worries they find difficult to discuss openly. This activity invites children to identify their clinical issues without having to verbalize them directly. Moreover, this activity provides rich assessment information pertaining to the child's underlying problems, as well as their intensity. The therapist can use the activity as a point of departure to elicit further information from the child. For example, if a child places a dot beside the statement, "I am worried about someone in my family," the therapist can ask, "Can you tell me more about these worries?"

The completed activity serves as a snapshot of the child's treatment issues, and assists the therapist in developing a treatment plan. As this is an assessment activity, the therapist's role is to gather information, not to intervene therapeutically. Therefore, as the child is completing the activity, the therapist should refrain from making any comments that would alter how the child completes the worksheet. For example, if the child places several dots beside the statement, "I do not like the way I look," indicating that the child has a negative self-image, the therapist should reflect and validate how the child feels, and not try to shift the child's thinking. Once the assessment has been completed, and the child is in treatment, the therapist can deal with any treatment issues that were identified during assessment.

Note: As this activity encourages the child to be open about his feelings and concerns, it may lead to a disclosure of abuse. Therefore, at the outset of the activity, the therapist should reinforce the rules about confidentiality, and the need to report any safety concerns. If the child discloses any safety concerns, the therapist must refrain from playing the investigative role. Rather, the therapist should follow reporting protocols and contact the local child protection authorities.

SURVEY

Everyone has problems and worries. This survey will help us understand what your problems and worries are, so we can help you. Read each statement below, and put a sticky-dot beside the statements that apply to you. You can put more sticky-dots if it's a bigger worry.

1. I CAN'T STOP THINKING ABOUT MY PROBLEMS

2. I FEEL SAD A LOT

3. I FEEL SCARED SOMETIMES

4. I FEEL LIKE I DID SOMETHING BAD

5. I DON'T LIKE THE WAY I LOOK

6. I AM WORRIED ABOUT GETTING HURT OR BEATEN UP

7. I AM WORRIED ABOUT SOMEONE IN MY FAMILY

8. I HAVE BAD DREAMS A LOT

9. I HAVE HEADACHES/STOMACH ACHES A LOT

10. I GET INTO BAD MOODS A LOT

11. I HURT MYSELF ON PURPOSE SOMETIMES

12. I THINK MY PARENTS ARE MAD AT ME

13. I GET INTO TROUBLE AT HOME A LOT

14. I GET INTO TROUBLE AT SCHOOL A LOT

15. I GET INTO FIGHTS WITH OTHER KIDS

16. I GET TEASED BY OTHER KIDS

17. I HAVE AN AWFUL SECRET I'M NERVOUS TO SHARE

18. SOMEBODY IS TOUCHING ME IN A WAY THAT I DON'T LIKE

19. I DON'T HAVE ANYONE TO TALK TO ABOUT MY WORRIES

20. I DON'T HAVE ANYTHING FUN TO DO AFTER SCHOOL OR ON WEEKENDS

SURVEY

Everyone has problems and worries. This survey will help us understand what your problems and worries are, so we can help you. Read each statement below, and put a sticky-dot beside the statements that apply to you. You can put more sticky-dots if it's a bigger worry.

1. I CAN'T STOP THINKING ABOUT MY PROBLEMS

2. I FIND IT DIFFICULT TO FEEL ANY JOY OR HAPPINESS

3. I FEEL I AM A BAD PERSON

4. I DON'T LIKE THE WAY I LOOK

5. I AM WORRIED ABOUT GETTING HURT OR BEATEN UP

6. I AM WORRIED ABOUT SOMEONE IN MY FAMILY

7. I HAVE TROUBLE SLEEPING

8. I HAVE HEADACHES/STOMACH ACHES A LOT

9. I DON'T FEEL LIKE EATING

10. I AM EATING A LOT MORE LATELY

11. I GET INTO BAD MOODS A LOT

12. I USE DRUGS OR ALCOHOL TO COPE WITH MY PROBLEMS

13. I TRY OR WANT TO HURT MYSELF

14. I FEEL LIKE MY LIFE WILL NEVER BE OKAY

15. I AM NOT GETTING ALONG WITH MY FAMILY

16. I AM NOT DOING WELL IN SCHOOL

17. I GET INTO FIGHTS WITH OTHER KIDS

18. I DO NOT FEEL COMFORTABLE WITH MY SEXUALITY

19. I HAVE AN AWFUL SECRET I'M NERVOUS TO SHARE

20. I DON'T HAVE ANYONE TO TALK TO ABOUT MY PROBLEMS

PUZZLE

Theme: Assessment
Recommended Age Range: 7-16
Treatment Modality: Individual, Group

Goals
1. Assess family relationships
2. Enable verbalization of feelings

Materials
• Paper
• Coloring supplies
• Puzzle (included)
• Envelopes
• Magazine pictures
• Scissors
• Tape

Advance Preparation
Copy the puzzle onto a piece of cardboard or heavy colored paper. Glue a magazine picture appropriate to the child's interests onto the other side. For example, a picture from a sports magazine might appeal to a child who enjoys sports, while another child might enjoy a picture of animals. Cut the puzzle along the dotted lines and place the eight pieces in an envelope.

Description
The therapist provides the child with a puzzle. The child completes the puzzle by writing a response to each of the eight questions. (If this activity is being used with younger children, the therapist can transcribe the child's statements.) The child completes the puzzle by writing a response to the first question and progressing to question eight. Once a response has been written for all eight questions, the child can assemble the puzzle and tape it together. The child can turn the puzzle over to uncover the picture. As an adjunct activity, the child can draw a family portrait.

Discussion
This activity gathers information related to family functioning and dynamics. The child's perception of his family is an important area to incorporate into the assessment. The puzzle and the family portrait provide significant diagnostic information, which are used as tools for further exploration. The exercises aid the treatment team in formulating goals for family intervention.

PUZZLE

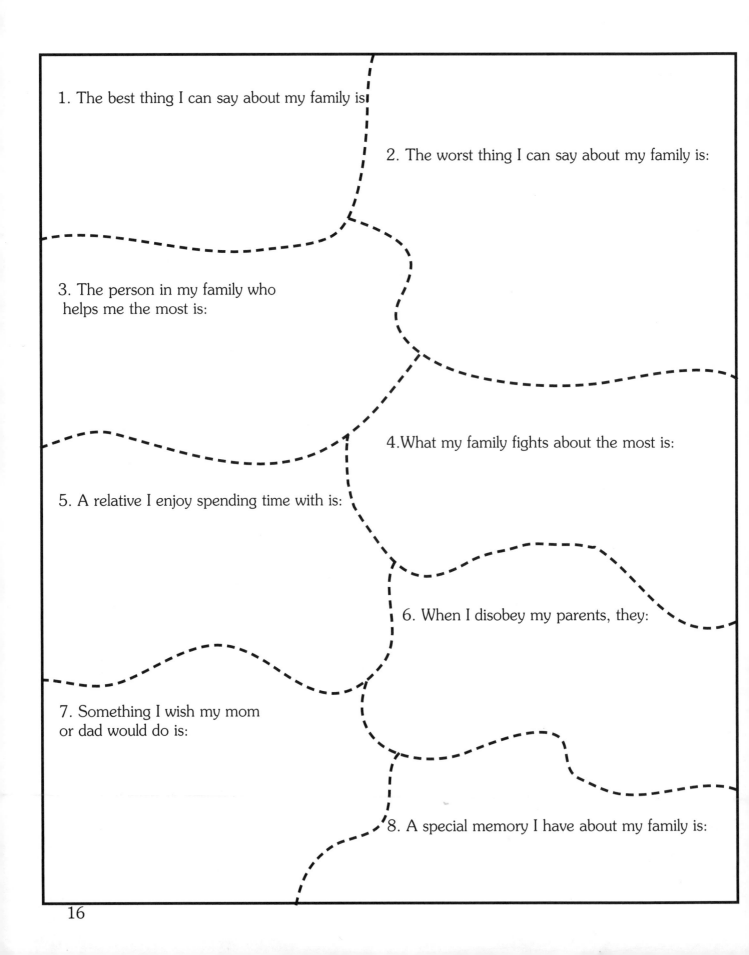

1. The best thing I can say about my family is:

2. The worst thing I can say about my family is:

3. The person in my family who helps me the most is:

4. What my family fights about the most is:

5. A relative I enjoy spending time with is:

6. When I disobey my parents, they:

7. Something I wish my mom or dad would do is:

8. A special memory I have about my family is:

LIFE'S UPS & DOWNS

Theme: Assessment
Recommended Age Range: 7-16
Treatment Modality: Individual

Goals
1. Assess significant events in the client's life
2. Help put positive and negative life events into perspective
3. Enable verbalization of feelings
4. Normalize that everyone has both positive and negative life experiences

Materials
- Masking tape
- Paper
- Writing and coloring supplies
- A large wall area (if one is unavailable, use a large area on the floor)

Description
Tape a long piece of masking tape across the wall, with ample space to stick the pieces of paper above and below the tape line. The therapist introduces the activity by explaining to the client that they are going to make a time line of important events in the client's life. The therapist asks the client to think back to his earliest memory, and write this memory down on one of the sheets of paper. If desired, the therapist can write for the client, or the client can draw the memory and have the therapist write a brief description of the memory underneath the client's picture. Ask the client to think about other significant events in his life, and write each one down on a separate sheet of paper. The therapist can guide the client through this process with questions such as, "Write about an important event in your life from when you were in grade one; from when you were in grade two" (and so on until the client reaches his current grade in school). If the client continues to have difficulty thinking of significant events, the therapist can break the activity down by asking additional questions, such as, "Write about a happy memory involving your family; write about an unhappy memory involving your family; write about a happy memory related to school; write about an unhappy memory related to school; write about a memory of one of your birthdays; write about a holiday you remember; write about a memory of when you accomplished something." Once the client has completed writing or drawing the memories and events, they are each taped to the wall. Positive events are taped above the line, negative events below the line. The therapist then guides the client to discuss in more detail each memory and his feelings associated with each memory. It is important for the therapist to emphasize that everyone experiences "ups and downs" in life.

Discussion
This activity is a valuable assessment tool, as it gathers information about significant events in the child's life. Some clients will enjoy completing this exercise, and will openly share their life experiences with the therapist. Other clients may struggle with the activity, because they may feel too anxious or ashamed to talk about their experiences. The therapist can deal with client resistance by making supportive comments that validate and normalize the client's feelings. If the therapist knows of significant

events in the client's life that the client has not included in the time line, the therapist should wait until the activity is completed, and then state, "Some memories may be too difficult for you to share right now. You can always add to your time line when you are feeling more comfortable."

In processing traumatic or difficult events in the client's life, it is important for the therapist to validate the client's resilience. For example, the therapist can state, "Even though you've been through a lot of tough times in your life, you're still here. . .you're a survivor!" The therapist can then ask, "What or who has helped you get through the tough times? How have the tough times made you a stronger person? How can you use this strength to get through any tough times you experience now or in the future?"

In addition to its diagnostic value, this activity can be used as a therapeutic intervention to facilitate discussion of various issues, such as change and loss, family relationships, and personal achievements.

CHAPTER TWO:
IDENTIFYING & EXPRESSING FEELINGS

Many children lack the emotional, cognitive and verbal abilities to communicate their feelings directly. Children may also suppress their feelings, or restrict their feelings vocabulary to "happy," "sad," and "mad." In such cases, children need permission to express themselves openly, and enhance their feelings vocabulary so they have a means of identifying a range of feeling states.

When children are limited in their ability to talk about their feelings, it can help to combine discussion with engaging play-based activities. The structured play activities in this chapter, such as board games, expressive arts techniques, and role-play exercises, help children verbalize and express their feelings with lowered levels of anxiety.

However, in order to do this work effectively, practitioners must be in-tune with their own emotions, and be able to express a range of feelings. This is essential if practitioners are to model the open identification and expression of affect. Practitioners also need to feel comfortable around children who display strong emotions, so they can normalize and validate children's feelings, and help them express themselves in a variety of healthy ways.

THE HOT POTATO GAME

Theme: Identifying and Expressing Feelings
Recommended Age Range: 4-10
Treatment Modality: Group, Family
Stage of Treatment: Beginning, Middle

Goals
1. Facilitate identification and discussion of feelings
2. Encourage greater awareness of feelings

Materials
• The Electronic Talking HOT POTATO (HOT POTATO © 1999 Hasbro. All Rights Reserved. Used with permission). (**Note:** The Electronic Talking HOT POTATO is a stuffed toy in the shape of a potato that plays music when squeezed. This is not the same as the MR. POTATO HEAD © toy, which is also a product of Hasbro. See resource section on page 111 for purchasing information.)
• Questions (included)
• Index cards or card stock

Advance Preparation
Copy each question from the HOT POTATO question card sheet onto separate index cards, or photocopy the question card sheet onto card stock and cut out each question.

Description
The group members sit in a circle, with the question cards placed in the middle of the circle. The leader asks the children if they have ever played the game HOT POTATO. The leader then shows the children the HOT POTATO toy, and then passes it around so they can become familiar with it. Stress that nobody is allowed to break the toy by pulling on it, or throwing it too hard. The leader explains the game as follows:

The leader squeezes the HOT POTATO stuffed toy and passes it to the person sitting to the left. The first person caught holding the HOT POTATO toy when the music stops answers the question that the leader reads aloud from the top of the question card pile. All the questions have to do with feelings. Children have the option of answering the question, passing, or asking the group for help. The game continues until all the questions have been answered. The following rules must be followed:

1. The 'potato' must be passed around the circle quickly. No one is allowed to hold onto it.
2. The 'potato' is passed, not thrown. If the 'potato' goes out of the circle, the last player who had it must get it, and continue passing it around the circle.
3. Only the child holding the 'potato' answers the question, so only one person is talking at a time.
4. The group leader is allowed to stop the game to discuss the feelings each child raises.

21

Discussion

Most children will already know how to play the HOT POTATO game. The activity will stimulate enthusiasm as the stuffed toy is passed around the group and will help the children talk about their feelings. As the game proceeds, the therapist provides supportive feedback and offers praise when group members take risks in verbalizing and expressing their thoughts and feelings. When a child openly discusses a painful or difficult event, the therapist validates the child's feelings and facilitates an appropriate but brief group discussion.

This game works well with pre-school and latency-aged children. They are eager to play with the stuffed toy, and use it as a tool to articulate and master their feelings. Withdrawn children typically become more animated as the game unfolds, while children who typically act out will become more contained as they are helped to play by the rules of the game and find acceptable ways to express their strong emotions.

Questions
THE HOT POTATO GAME

Show with your face and body what someone looks like when he is happy.	**Show with your face and body what someone looks like when he is sad.**
Show with your face and body what someone looks like when he is mad.	**Show with your face and body what someone looks like when he is scared.**
What makes you feel happy?	**What makes you feel sad?**
What makes you feel mad?	**What makes you feel scared?**
How would you feel if your brother or sister broke your favorite toy?	**How would you feel if another girl or boy did not want to play with you?**
How would you feel if you woke up from a bad dream?	**How would you feel if someone said something nice to you?**

THE CANDY LAND GAME

Theme: Identifying and Expressing Feelings
Recommended Age Range: 6-12
Treatment Modality: Individual, Group, Family
Stage of Treatment: Beginning, Middle

Goals

1. Facilitate identification and expression of feelings
2. Enhance coping skills

Materials

• The CANDY LAND Game (CANDY LAND ® is a Trademark of Hasbro. © 1999 Hasbro. All Rights Reserved. Used with permission.)
• Candy prizes: mints, lollipops, gummy bears, jellybeans (enough for each player)
• Three gift bags or zip lock bags for candy prizes
• Three labels
• Small treasure chest or box

Advance Preparation

Set aside one jellybean to use as the game marker and fill the small treasure chest with the remaining jellybeans before placing it on the game board, covering the "Candy Castle." Remove the plastic gingerbread men that come with the game, as they will not be needed.

Set aside the candy cane, gumdrop and lollipop picture cards that come with the game for placement in the stack of cards. These cards correspond with the candy prizes. Remove the other two picture cards that come with the game, as they will not be needed.

Prepare the following labels and insert one in each of the candy prize bags:

MAD MINTS! We all get mad sometimes. Give a mint candy to each player who shares a safe way to cope with mad feelings.
GRUMPY GUMMY BEARS! We all get grumpy sometimes. Give a gummy bear to each player who shares a way to cope with grumpy feelings.
LAUGHING LOLLIPOPS! Laughing makes us feel good. Give a lollipop to each player who makes you laugh.

Set aside one yellow, one blue, and one red colored square cardboard card from the stack of cards that comes with the game. On each of these three cards, color a black dot in the middle of the color block. On the corresponding blank side, write:

(Yellow) Sometimes when children don't get their own way, they sulk or pout. Show what people look like when they are pouting. What's a better way to show you're upset?
(Blue) Pretend you're at the store and your parent won't buy you a treat, so you throw a tantrum. What's a better way to show you're upset?
(Red) Pretend that you and your sister are watching TV and she keeps changing the channel, so

you get mad and hit her. What's a better way to deal with your mad feelings?

Set aside one of each of the six colored square cardboard cards and write the following under-neath the appropriate square:

(Red) Mad
(Blue) Sad
(Orange) Worried
(Purple) Scared
(Green) Guilty
(Yellow) Happy

Place these cards beside the game board for use during the game so players know which feel-ings correspond to which colors. The remaining colored cards will be placed in a stack on the game board and used to direct players along the path, and to prompt players to talk about times when they experienced these feelings.

In order to move the game along more quickly, pre-arrange the cards. Of course, the number of cards used and the order in which they are placed will depend on the number of turns the leader wishes each player to have. The following is designed for four children each having five turns:
1. One purple block
2. One green block
3. Candy cane picture card
4. Two red blocks
5. One orange block
6. Gum drop picture card
7. One yellow block with black dot
8. One green block
9. Two yellow blocks
10. One red block
11. Two green blocks
12. One blue block with black dot
13. Two orange blocks
14. Lollipop picture card
15. Two yellow blocks
16. One red block with black dot
17. One blue block
18. One green block
19. One orange block
20. One purple block

Description
The leader begins by defining the various feelings (mad, sad, worried, scared, guilty, happy.) An example for each feeling state is given, to ensure the children understand the definitions. Next, the leader asks if anyone has ever played the CANDY LAND game (most children are familiar with the game and will respond to this question with enthusiasm). The leader states that the group is going to play a special version of the CANDY LAND game, and explains the rules as follows:

To begin, place a jellybean at the start space on the game board. The jellybean is the game piece that moves along the board. The youngest player draws a card and moves the jellybean ahead to the space indicated. For example, if the card has one color block, move the jellybean to the first matching space; if the card has two color blocks, move the jellybean to the second matching space; if the card has a picture, move the jellybean to the matching picture; if the card has a color block with a black dot, move the jellybean to the matching color space with the black dot. When a player lands on a colored space, he tells about a time he felt the feeling depicted by the card. For example, a red space means the player talks about a time he felt mad. When a player picks a card with a colored space that has a black dot on it, he moves the jellybean to the colored space on the board with the black dot and follows the instructions on the back of the card. When a player picks a special card (a card with a picture on it), he moves the jellybean to the corresponding picture space on the path, opens the corresponding prize bag, follows the instructions on the label, and shares the prize with the group. The game continues with players following the appropriate instructions at each turn. The player who reaches the end first, opens the jellybean treasure and shares the jellybeans with the other children.

As the game proceeds, the group leader facilitates by helping the children talk about their feelings. The leader can play along with the rest of the group and model the appropriate expression of affect.

Variation for individual therapy: The game is played as above, but the cards are ordered in such a way to make the game go faster, i.e. the lollipop picture card can be stacked closer to the top of the pile so that the jellybean jumps quickly along the path.

Discussion

The CANDY LAND game is a favorite board game among young children. The modification of the CANDY LAND game to a therapeutic game is intended to engage children in the treatment process and help them verbalize their feelings. The therapist can use the game as a point of departure to normalize feeling states and to stress the importance of affect expression. The candy treats, as well as the action cards add to the appeal of the activity, and further facilitate the appropriate expression of affect. The element of competition from the original version of the CANDY LAND game is removed, as the group members must work cooperatively to move the jellybean along the path to the treasure. Moreover, everyone playing the game is a winner, as the jellybeans are shared among all the players.

FINGER PAINTS

Theme: Identifying and Expressing Feelings
Recommended Age Range: 4-16
Treatment Modality: Individual, Group, Family
Stage of Treatment: Beginning, Middle

Goals
1. Facilitate identification and expression of feelings
2. Normalize that people experience a range of feelings
3. Encourage awareness of feelings

Materials
- Finger paints in assorted colors
- Large sheets of white paper
- Smock
- Newspaper or garbage bags

Advance Preparation
Prepare by laying the finger paints out on a table, and covering the surrounding floor with newspaper or garbage bags.

Description
The therapist provides the child with paper and finger paints. The child can have time at the beginning to paint freely in order to become comfortable with the use of the paint medium. The therapist then asks the child the following:

Paint a picture to show me how you are feeling right now.
Paint a picture that will tell a story about a time when you felt happy.
Paint a picture that will tell a story about a time when you felt sad, scared or yucky.
Paint a picture that will tell a story about another time when you felt happy.

After the child has completed the pictures, ask the child to discuss them, to compare them, or to tell a story about each one. The pictures can be used to facilitate further discussion regarding positive and negative experiences in the child's life. The emphasis should be on what happened and how the child felt. It is important to end with a "happy" picture, so positive feelings are brought to the surface at the end of the session.

Discussion
Children's artwork can be used in clinical sessions as tools for projective testing and creative expression. Through the expressive arts medium, the child's thoughts, feelings, and experiences can be translated into concrete images. The finger paints facilitate cathartic release and help children to externalize their trauma. The role of the therapist is to help the child translate his picture into words, so he can communicate his feelings and gain a sense of mastery.

Note: The therapist should not interpret the child's artwork unless he is a trained art therapist.

However, this is not to say that the therapist cannot use the child's artwork to gather information and to help the child express his feelings. Instead of interpreting for the child, ask him to tell you about his picture.

BASKETBALL

Theme: Identifying and Expressing Feelings
Recommended Age Range: 7-16
Treatment Modality: Individual, Group, Family
Stage of Treatment: Middle

Goals
1. Facilitate identification and expression of feelings
2. Normalize that people experience both positive and negative life events

Materials
• NERF BASKETBALL (NERF ® is a Trademark of Hasbro. © 1999 Hasbro. All Rights Reserved. Used with permission). Alternatively, a garbage can and crumpled paper can be used.
• Questions (included)
• Blue and yellow index cards or card stock

Advance Preparation
Copy each "Happy Face" question from the BASKETBALL question card sheet onto yellow index cards, and draw a happy face on the reverse side of each card. Copy each "Sad Face" question from the Basketball question card sheet onto blue index cards, and draw a sad face on the reverse side of each card.

Description
Explain to the group that they are going to play a special kind of basketball, which will help them to discuss happy and sad feelings. The rules are explained as follows:

Players take turns shooting a basket. If a player successfully throws the ball through the basketball hoop, he picks a card from the "happy face" pile. These questions relate to happy experiences in a person's life. If a player misses the basket, he picks a card from the "sad face" pile. These questions relate to unhappy experiences in a person's life. The player can choose to answer that question, pass, or ask the group for help. The game continues until all the questions have been answered, or until each player has had a pre-chosen number of turns. If all of the question cards have been answered before the game is over, the pile of cards can be shuffled and re-used.

Active discussion between the group members is encouraged during the game. The therapist may wish to stop the game periodically to expand on feelings or issues disclosed by the group members.

Variation for individual therapy: The child and therapist take turns as above. During the game, the therapist can respond by reflecting the child's feelings and, where appropriate, by asking the child to elaborate. The therapist can tailor his responses to model and encourage open disclosure, or draw the child closer to specific treatment issues. This should be done gradually and with sensitivity to the child's readiness to deal with salient issues.

Discussion

Modifying the traditional game of basketball can help otherwise resistant clients openly identify and express their feelings. The therapist can use this game to assess the child's feelings, attitudes, and style of interaction, and to intervene therapeutically when the child is being emotionally guarded, oppositional, or socially inappropriate. The "happy" and "sad" question cards can be used to enable the child to become aware of and express both positive and negative feelings and experiences.

In a group context, the therapist can normalize and validate the experiences of the group members by asking questions, such as, "Has this happened to anyone else here?" "Who else in this group has felt this way?" "What do others in the group think about what was just said?" As the group members answer the questions, the therapist can offer praise and encouragement by saying, "You were brave to have talked about that," or "You are doing a great job sharing your feelings with the group!" The therapist can reinforce appropriate social interaction throughout the game; for instance, "Everyone is doing such a good job of listening to each other!"

During the game, group members are given the option of passing on their turn so they do not feel pressured to discuss issues beyond their emotional readiness. In this way, group members can be encouraged to share information at a pace that feels safe and comfortable.

Questions
BASKETBALL

Happy Face Cards

Tell about the happiest moment of your life.	Tell about a happy memory you have from when you were very little.
Tell about a time someone did something nice for you.	Tell about something you have accomplished.
Tell about a time you and your family did something fun together.	Tell about a time you did something brave.
Tell about a good dream you had.	Tell about something that makes you laugh.
What's the best thing that's happened to you this week?	Tell about a time you were able to solve a problem you had.

Sad Face Cards

Tell about a sad moment in your life.	What would you say to a child who was smiling all the time, when you know he is really sad?
What is your biggest worry?	Tell about a bad dream that you had.
Tell about a time someone did something that upset you.	When was the last time you cried? What happened that made you so upset?
Tell about a problem you are having at school.	Tell about a problem you had this week.
Tell about a problem you are having at home.	What is something you would like to work on or improve about yourself?

FEELINGS BLOW-OUT

Theme: Identifying and Expressing Feelings
Recommended Age Range: 4-16
Treatment Modality: Individual, Group, Family
Stage of Treatment: Middle

Goals

1. Facilitate identification and expression of feelings
2. Normalize that people experience a range of feelings
3. Teach deep-breathing relaxation techniques
4. Strengthen impulse control and self-regulation abilities

Materials

• BLOPENS (BLOPENS ® are used with the kind permission of P&M Products Ltd., Redhill, Surrey RH1 3LX UK. BLOPENS are a Trademark of P&M Products Ltd.) These special markers spray colored ink when air is blown into them. See resource section on page 111 for purchasing information. (**Note:** If this activity is being used with a group of children, mouth-pieces should be attached to the BLOPENS to avoid passing along germs. See the resource section at the back of this book for further information.)
• Large sheets of white paper

Description

The therapist gives a brief demonstration of how the BLOPENS work, then, under supervision, the child takes a few minutes to practice. The child is instructed to assign a feeling to each colored BLOPEN, e.g. blue = sad, red = mad, yellow = happy, and so on. A grid showing which color represents each feeling may be helpful.

The child then selects one colored BLOPEN to begin, sprays the colored ink onto the paper by blowing into the pen, states which feeling the color represents, and discusses a time when he felt that feeling. The child can spray more of one color to illustrate intense feelings, and may say for example, "Blue is for sad. I felt sad when my mom and dad got a divorce. I'm spraying a lot of blue because I felt very sad." The child can create colorful designs by spraying the colors in various directions onto the paper. As the child is doing this, the therapist can provide positive feedback by making comments, such as, "I see you have a lot of sad feelings inside. You're doing a great job of getting your feelings out!"

In addition to helping the child identify different feeling states, the BLOPENS can be used for other therapeutic purposes:
>   1. Relaxation/deep-breathing exercises: To demonstrate, therapist takes a deep breath, then slowly breathes out into the BLOPEN, controlling the spray of ink.
>   2. Expression of feelings: As the child is blowing into the pen, the therapist can ask, "How do you feel when you blow into the pen?" The child will likely respond by saying it feels "good" or "fun." The therapist can then comment that people usually feel better when they let their feelings out.

3. Development of better impulse control: The therapist purposely sprays the ink haphazardly all over the paper, and then states, "Look what happens when I have no control over what I'm doing, and I spray the ink all over. It gets very messy. It's better if I think about my color design first, then carefully spray the ink on the paper."

Variation for younger children: This activity can be simplified for use with younger children as follows: Have the child select four different colored BLOPENS. Explain that one BLOPEN will be for "happy" feelings, one for "sad" feelings, one for "mad" feelings, and one for "scared" feelings. Explain each feeling using examples the child will understand. Ask the child to give examples of when he experienced feeling each emotion. Then have the child create a design with the BLOPENS by spraying the colored ink onto the paper.

Discussion
Expressive arts can be a powerful tool in helping children externalize their feelings in a constructive manner. "Feelings blow-out" is an expressive arts technique that provides information for diagnosis and assessment, facilitates the child's healthy release of emotion, and promotes self-expression. During the exercise, the therapist observes the child's use of the BLOPENS, selection of colors, sequence of feeling states, and behavioral presentation. The child develops a feeling of safety by setting the pace and controlling which feelings and experiences he wishes to discuss. The therapist can reinforce the fact that any of these feelings is acceptable. Most children will enjoy this craft activity and will become easily engaged in the therapeutic process.

Note: The therapist should not interpret the child's artwork unless he is a trained art therapist. This is not to say that the therapist cannot use the child's artwork to gather information and to help the child express his feelings. Rather than interpreting the art, ask the child to tell you about his picture.

FEELINGS TIC TAC TOE

Theme: Identifying and Expressing Feelings
Recommended Age Range: 7-16
Treatment Modality: Individual, Group, Family
Stage of Treatment: Beginning, Middle

Goals
1. Facilitate identification and expression of feelings

Materials
• "Feelings tic tac toe" worksheet (included)
• Score card (included)
• 2 kinds of wrapped candy (about the size of a nickel or quarter)

Description
This game of tic-tac-toe uses candy instead of X's and O's. It can be used in either individual counseling, with the therapist playing, or in pairs of children at similar levels of functioning.

Players alternately place their candy pieces on the work/game sheet provided in an attempt to get either an uninterrupted horizontal, vertical, or diagonal line of three. Once a player gets a line, he must uncover the feeling faces in the line and describe a time when he experienced each of those three feelings. If he talks about all three feelings, he gets a point. If no player gets a straight line, nobody gets a point for that round. Once a player accumulates five points, he gets to eat one of the candies. The therapist can pre-set a time limit for the activity.

Discussion
Most clients are familiar with tic-tac-toe and will enjoy this version of the game. Children are generally able to understand the concept of feeling happy, sad, or mad. Other feelings, such as guilt or jealousy, need to be explained using examples that the child will understand. For example, "Guilty means feeling bad about what you did. Like, if you cheat on a test, you would feel guilty when you realize that you did something wrong." Once the child comprehends each of the feelings on the game board, he is better able to ascribe feelings to situations in his own life. As the child talks about his feelings, the therapist can reflect the child's feelings, ask the child to elaborate, and praise the child for his openness. For example, the therapist can say to the child, "I'm glad you felt comfortable enough talking about your sad feelings when your mom died. It took a lot of guts to share that, so you really earned that point!" When it is the therapist's turn to share, the therapist can tailor his own responses in a way that would be therapeutically beneficial to the child.

FEELINGS TIC TAC TOE

Happy

Mad

Nervous

Scared

Loved

Guilty

Jealous

Sad

Relieved

Feelings Tic Tac Toe Score Sheet

On the score sheet below, write the name of each player in the space provided.
Put a check mark (✓) when a player wins a point.

Name:	Name:

CHAPTER THREE
COPING WITH FEELINGS

Many children use maladaptive strategies to cope with their strong emotions. Feelings of sadness, anger, guilt or anxiety can be particularly difficult to deal with. If children do not learn healthy ways to cope with their feelings, then they are at risk for developing serious difficulties, such as depression or violent behavior. In this chapter, interventions are used to help children express feelings, manage anger, and cope with stress.

In selecting an activity from this chapter, the practitioner should consider the therapeutic goals for the child. For example, if a young child is experiencing difficulty with the appropriate expression of anger, then the clay activity can be a useful intervention. If a child is struggling with feelings of guilt and shame, then perhaps he would bene-fit from the TROUBLE® game. If the therapist is working with a client who is exhibiting self-harming behavior, then the comfort kit can be a helpful intervention. In general, the six activities in this chapter provide children with opportunities to learn and practice healthy coping styles, so they can deal more effectively with overwhelming experiences.

STUFFED ANIMALS

Theme: Coping With Feelings
Recommended Age Range: 4-10
Treatment Modality: Individual
Stage of Treatment: Middle

Goals
1. Facilitate identification and expression of feelings
2. Enhance problem-solving skills and coping strategies
3. Strengthen support systems

Materials
• Stuffed animals
• Stories (included)

Description
The therapist selects one of the stories provided, reads it to the child, and solicits input at various designated points in the story. At the end of the activity, the child can make up his or her own story, using the stuffed animals and any other available props.

Discussion
The use of storytelling in child therapy is a valuable therapeutic tool. Repetitive themes in the story tap into the child's unconscious, and thereby effect change. The therapist can adapt each story to mirror the child's situation and encourage the child to verbalize feelings and enhance problem-solving abilities. Children with more limited problem-solving abilities may need additional guidance from the therapist. For example, options can be provided for the child to choose from, such as, "Do you think the little bunny should get into a big fight with the other bunnies, should he ignore them, or should he tell them that it is not nice to be a tease?"

The stuffed animals add to the appeal of the activity, as children naturally gravitate to them, and use them to elicit affective projection. As the focus is on the stuffed animal, attention is shifted away from the child. This increases the child's comfort level and enables him to explore feelings and issues from a safe distance. The therapist facilitates the treatment process by engaging the child to "help" the stuffed animal. By "helping" the stuffed animal, the child indirectly addresses his own emotional needs.

The Little Bunny

Once there was a bunny named ___. This bunny lived in the forest with his family. He liked to play and have fun, but nobody would play with him. The other bunnies wouldn't play with him because he was ___. The other bunnies made fun of him a lot. They laughed at him, and called him mean names, like ___ and ___. This made him feel very ___. Sometimes, when the other bunnies were teasing him, he would try to say something, but then he would feel too shy, so he just kept quiet. Sometimes, he would feel so upset, he would

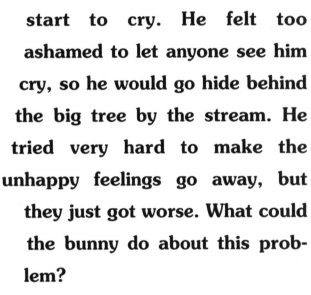 start to cry. He felt too ashamed to let anyone see him cry, so he would go hide behind the big tree by the stream. He tried very hard to make the unhappy feelings go away, but they just got worse. What could the bunny do about this problem?

The Little Fish

Once there was a little fish named ___. She lived in the ocean under a beautiful coral reef. She loved to swim and play with the other sea animals. Sometimes she and her friends would play hide and seek in the shells, or play tag among the big, tall bushes of seaweed. There was plenty to eat, and there were beautiful sea gardens to explore. The water was always calm and there were no worries. These were happy times that made her feel ___. But one day, there was a terrible storm. The stormy waters tossed about the little fish and the beautiful gardens were thrown violently by the heavy waves. It was such a frightening experience. After what seemed like a very long time, the storm died down. The little fish looked around and saw that everything had been destroyed. The seashells were all cracked, the sea weed bushes broken, and the beautiful sea gardens were demolished. There was very little food left to eat. The little fish felt so ___. After a while, the little fish decided there was no use in just feeling sorry for herself, so she came up with a plan about what to do. She gathered her friends together and said: ____.

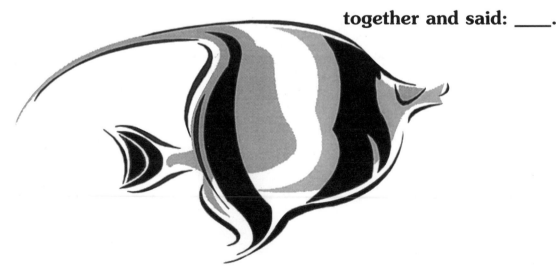

The Kitten

Once there was a kitten named ___. She lived in a pet store, with her parents, and her brothers and sisters. Her favorite part of the day was feeding time, when she would get to snuggle against the warm soft belly of her mommie and drink the smooth, sweet milk. Then the kitten would curl up with her brothers and sisters in a little bundle against their mommies tummy, and fall into a deep, peaceful sleep. The kitten would have wonderful dreams about ___. One day, after the kitten woke up from her nap, she noticed that one of her brothers was missing. She didn't know where he had gone, so she felt ___. The next day, the same thing happened, but this time, it was her sister that went missing. After a few days, only she and her mommie were left. She noticed that her mommie looked very sad and worried, and this made the kitten feel even more ___. The kitten started to hate naptime, because she was now having terrible dreams about ___. Another two days went by, and then something really awful happened. The kitten woke up from her nap, and her mommie was gone! She was all alone. She felt so ___. What could this kitten do to feel better?

The Little Pig

Once there was a little pig named ___. He lived on a farm with his family and his friends. His best friend was Cookie the cow. He called her cookie because she was covered with brown spots that looked like peanut butter cookies! This little pig and his best friend Cookie would run in the fields, jump in the hay, and roll in the mud. They laughed and played all day long! Their favorite game was ___. They would stay out and play for as along as they could, because the little pig didn't like to go home. Things were not very happy at home because his parents were fighting all the time, his big brother picked on him a lot, and it was just so noisy all the time. The little pig would try and stay in his room where it was a little quieter, but he could still hear the fighting going on. Sometimes he would hear doors slamming, loud thumps and crashing noises. Then he would hear his mom crying. This would make him feel very ___. The little pig wondered if perhaps there was someone he could talk to about this problem. So the next day, instead of going down to the haystack where he usually met Cookie to play, he went to talk to ___. He wasn't sure exactly what to say, but finally he mustered up all his courage, and said: ___. He felt much better once he was able to talk about what was troubling him, and he got some very good advice. He was told to ___.

CLAY

Theme: Coping With Feelings
Recommended Age Range: 4-10
Treatment Modality: Individual, Group, Family
Stage of Treatment: Middle

Goals

1. Facilitate identification and expression of anger
2. Normalize that everyone experiences anger
3. Teach appropriate anger-management skills

Materials

• Clay

Description

Give the child some clay and some time to play with it. Then explain that the clay is going to be used to help talk about "mad feelings." The therapist and the child can each give examples of the kinds of situations that make people feel mad. The therapist guides the child through the following five tasks:

Task #1: The therapist asks the child to make a happy face with the clay and describe a time when he felt happy. Next, the therapist asks the child to make a mad face with the clay, and describe a time when he felt mad. The therapist and the child then have a contest, taking turns to see who can make the maddest looking face.

Task #2: The therapist asks the child to make a little boy/girl out of the clay, and tell a story about this person based on the following. The therapist and child take turns adding to the story:

Once there was a little boy/girl. This little boy/girl loved to play ____ and eat ___ and watch ___ on TV. This little boy/girl felt happy when ____. Sometimes, this little boy/girl would get very mad, like when ___. When this would happen, the little boy/girl would ___. After the little boy/girl talked to a grown-up about why he/she was so mad, he/she felt much better. The end!"

Task #3: The therapist asks the child to make a big blob with the clay, and to pound it with his fist ten times. Explain that it is okay to feel mad but it is not okay to show your mad feelings by hurting someone else or by hurting yourself. Mad feelings can be let out by punching the clay or by punching a soft pillow.

The therapist and the child can take turns to see who can pound the clay the hardest.

Task #4: The therapist asks the child to pretend to have a tantrum with the clay by throwing it about on the floor. The therapist explains that sometimes, when children don't get what they want, they have a tantrum, but having a tantrum only makes things worse. So what can children do instead of having a tantrum when they feel mad? The therapist and the child make up a list of coping strategies together.

Task #5: The therapist asks the child to pretend to have a fight with the clay by making two blobs and smashing them against each other. The therapist explains that sometimes, when children get mad, they let out their mad feelings by getting into a fight, but that just gets them into more trouble, and then they feel more upset. So what can children do when they get mad, instead of getting into a fight? The child can select from the list of coping strategies that he and the therapist devised in Task #4.

Once the child has completed the five tasks, he can be given time to play with the clay. As a closing activity, the therapist and the child can play charades with the clay, taking turns to mold objects for the other person to guess.

Discussion

Children will become easily engrossed in this activity, as they shape, form, alter and destroy the clay, and use it as an outlet for aggressive feelings. Withdrawn children who internalize their feelings can use this activity to gradually express suppressed anger while children who externalize their feelings can learn more appropriate techniques to manage their anger. Throughout the activity, there is ample opportunity for the therapist to model the appropriate expression of anger.

THE TROUBLE GAME

Theme: Coping With Feelings
Recommended Age Range: 7-16
Treatment Modality: Individual, Group
Stage of Treatment: Middle

Goals
1. Normalize situations in which children typically feel guilty
2. Enable verbalization of guilty feelings
3. Enhance problem-solving skills
4. Challenge and correct feelings of guilt and shame

Materials
• The TROUBLE game (TROUBLE ® and POP-O-MATIC ® are Trademarks of Hasbro. ©1999 Hasbro. All Rights Reserved. Used with permission.) (Can be purchased at toy stores in the board game section.)
• Scenarios (included)
• Index cards or card stock
• Balloons
• Pennies
• Prizes

Advance Preparation
Select the appropriate scenarios from the list provided and copy each onto a separate index card or photocopy the scenarios sheet onto card stock and cut out each scenario. Modify to suit age and treatment needs where necessary.

Description
The leader begins the session by facilitating a discussion about children's feelings of guilt and shame. The leader can state, "Guilt means feeling bad about what you did and shame means feeling bad about who you are. Everyone experiences feelings of guilt and shame sometimes, but children who get into trouble a lot might believe they are a bad person." The group members can offer examples of when they experienced feelings of guilt and shame.

The leader then states that the group is going to play a game that will help them discuss feelings of guilt and shame. The leader asks if they have ever played the TROUBLE game (many will be familiar with the game) and then explains the following differences in the game:

Each player selects one of the four different colored pegs. Each player places his or her peg in the matching "home base" space located on the game unit. The player who pops the highest number with the POP-O-MATIC dice shaker goes first. If an even number is popped, move the peg out of the home base the appropriate number of spaces and around the game board clockwise. If an odd number is popped, select a question card, instead of moving a peg, and read it before responding. There are two types of question cards: STAY OUT OF TROUBLE CARDS and DON'T FEEL BAD CARDS. These cards all have to do with situations in which kids typically feel like they have done something bad or caused trouble (that's why the name of the game is TROUBLE!) There are also TREAT CARDS to make the game more fun and TAKE A BREAK CARDS to make the game more active. Players are awarded a token when they answer a question card. The first player to move his peg completely around the board and back into home base gets 3 extra tokens. The tokens are traded in at the end of the game for prizes.

3-10 tokens = 1 prize
11-20 tokens = 2 prizes
21 or more tokens = 3 prizes

Variation for individual therapy: The therapist and child play against each other. The therapist uses the game to initiate discussions about "feeling guilty or bad" and to model appropriate problem-solving skills.

Discussion

Many children struggle with feelings of guilt and shame. When children internalize the message that they are "bad," their acting out behavior often escalates, as this is a way for them to express how they feel. It is, therefore, important for children to work through their feelings of guilt within a safe therapeutic environment. Within the context of the game, there are many opportunities for the therapist to challenge and correct cognitive distortions that lead to feelings of guilt, and to convey therapeutic messages, including:

– *Just because somebody makes a poor decision does not mean that he is bad.*
– *Nobody deserves to be abused.*
– *Our wishes, thoughts, and words do not make bad things happen.*
– *Everyone is capable of making good decisions.*

SCENARIOS
TROUBLE

Stay Out of Trouble Card
Derek got into trouble for beating up a kid who called him a loser. You get a token if you can identify a more appropriate way for Derek to handle his anger.

Stay Out of Trouble Card
Sam liked the attention he got from being the class clown, but his behavior got him into trouble from his teacher. You get a token if you can identify a more appropriate way for Sam to get attention.

Stay Out of Trouble Card
Nick kept getting into trouble for forgetting his homework. You get a token if you can come up with some ideas to help Nick remember his homework.

Stay Out of Trouble Card
Abdul often got into trouble for not stopping to think before he acted. You get a token if you can identify a way to help Abdul with this problem.

Stay Out of Trouble Card
Willy and his family were driving to go visit relatives. Willy got in trouble for fighting in the back seat with his brother. You get a token if you can identify a way for Willy to handle himself better and stay out of trouble.

Stay Out of Trouble Card
Betty gets into trouble for day dreaming in class. You get a token if you can identify ways for Betty to pay attention.

Stay Out of Trouble Card
Mark got into trouble for skipping school with his friends. Mark didn't want to skip school but he felt pressured by his friends. You get a token if you can identify a way for Mark to handle this peer pressure.

Stay Out of Trouble Card
Lynn got angry when her parents wouldn't let her go to the mall so she trashed her room. You get a token if you can identify a more appropriate way for Lynn to handle this.

Treat Card
Give each player a lucky penny as a reminder that you are not a bad person and you deserve to have good things happen to you.

Treat Card
Give each player a balloon to celebrate what a great kid you are!

SCENARIOS
TROUBLE

Don't Feel Bad Card

Shane thought his parents took him to see a therapist because he is bad. Discuss.

Don't Feel Bad Card

Daniel thought it was his fault that his mother got beaten up by his dad, because he didn't do anything to stop it. Discuss.

Don't Feel Bad Card

Steven was playing in the living room and accidentally knocked over a vase and broke it. His mother got very angry and beat him. Steven thought he deserved this punishment because he was bad. Discuss.

Don't Feel Bad Card

Brian got into a fight with his dad. Later that day, his father was in a car accident and died. Brian felt the accident was all his fault. Discuss.

Don't Feel Bad Card

Amy got sexually abused by her uncle. She felt it was her fault because she didn't say no. Discuss.

Don't Feel Bad Card

Lisa has a learning disability and struggles to keep up in class. This makes her feel like a bad kid. Discuss.

Stay Out of Trouble Card

Risa's mother died of AIDS. Risa blamed herself because she thought she should have done a better job taking care of her mother. Discuss.

Stay Out of Trouble Card

Jeff's parents were fighting all the time and they finally got a divorce. Jeff blamed himself for the divorce because a lot of the fights were about him. Discuss.

Take a Break!

Do 10 jumping jacks

Take a Break!

Jog on the spot for 1 minute

A LOT ON MY PLATE

Theme: Coping With Feelings
Recommended Age Range: 9-16
Treatment Modality: Individual, Group, Family
Stage of Treatment: Middle

Goals
1. Enable identification of stresses
2. Enhance problem-solving skills and coping strategies
3. Normalize that stress is a part of life

Materials
- Paper plates (one per client)
- Pieces of paper, cut into strips (about ten strips for each client)
- Pencils or markers

Description
Begin by brainstorming a list of problems and worries. The therapist normalizes that everyone experiences stress. The therapist then provides the client with a paper plate, blank paper strips, and a pencil. The client identifies personal concerns or worries and writes each one down on a separate paper strip. The client loads the "problem" strips onto the paper plate; thus the metaphor, "I have a lot on my plate."

The client and therapist discuss each of the problems, and brainstorm ways to cope with them. Once a suitable coping strategy has been identified for a particular problem, that problem strip is removed from the plate. The end of the exercise should leave the client with a "lighter load" on the plate.

The therapist can emphasize that when people feel overwhelmed by their problems, it is often helpful to break each problem down and deal with each concern separately. The therapist can also point out that people usually feel less overwhelmed when they are able to talk about their problems, and identify effective ways to cope.

Discussion
"A Lot on My Plate" is a concrete tool that helps clients identify and manage their life stresses. In addition to providing the client with strategies to cope with current concerns, future problems can be circumvented by providing the client with tools to deal with anticipated problems. For example, the therapist can ask the client to think of an upcoming stressful time or event, such as an exam, and to think of how to apply the coping strategies identified in this session to the anticipated situation. This process will provide the client with a means to prevent the exacerbation of problems, and maintain a sense of control over life stresses.

DARTS

Theme: Coping With Feelings
Recommended Age Range: 9-16
Treatment Modality: Individual, Group
Stage of Treatment: Middle

Goals
1. Encourage positive coping strategies
2. Enhance problem-solving skills

Materials
- Child-safe dart game, such as one with foam darts
- Masking tape
- Paper and pen
- Questions (included)
- Index cards or card stock
- Stress balls (one per child)
- Gift bag and gift tag

Advance Preparation
Fill the gift bag with the stress balls and attach the following message:

Everyone in this group is a winner because you all did a great job talking about ways to cope with your feelings! You are being rewarded for your efforts with these stress balls. You can squeeze the ball when you are upset as a way to handle your stress.

The target is hung on the wall. A line is made on the floor with masking tape to establish the throwing distance from the target.

Select the appropriate questions from the question card sheet, and copy each question onto a separate index card or photocopy the question card sheet onto card stock and cut out each question. Modify to suit age and treatment needs where necessary.

Description
The group begins by brainstorming a list of positive coping strategies. Next, the leader explains that the group is going to play a special version of darts that will help the group discuss ways to deal with problems and manage stress. The leader outlines the dart game as follows:

Players take turns standing behind the tapeline, and throwing a dart at the target. The leader records each player's score. After each turn, the player draws a question from the stack of index cards, and reads the question aloud to the group. That player can choose to answer the question, pass, or ask the group for help. The game ends when all of the questions have been answered, or until a pre-designated time has elapsed. The player with the highest score at the end of the game can open the gift bag, read the message on the gift tag, and distribute the prize to the group.

Discussion

More often than not, troubled children resist discussing their problems and concerns. They have limited solutions for dealing with negative emotions, conflict, and stress. The target game attracts the interest of children and helps them develop their repertoire of adaptive coping strategies. It provides the leader with the opportunity to provoke discussion and to facilitate the open exchange of ideas. Although the game is designed as a therapeutic tool, it also gives children the opportunity to play and have fun.

Questions
DARTS

Laughing is a great stress release! What is something that makes you laugh?

It is important to find safe ways to express angry feelings. Identify a safe way to vent your anger.

Crying is a healthy way to express your sadness. Tell about a time when you cried.

It is important to take care of your body. What are three things you can do to take care of your body?

Talking to a trusted adult is a great way to get support for yourself. Who is someone you can talk to?

Without using words, show what you look like when you are feeling angry. What helps calm you down when you are feeling angry?

Everyone has bad dreams sometimes. What is something you can do to feel better if you wake up from a bad dream?

Getting into fights with other people only makes things worse. What is a safe way to deal with people who bother you?

Everyone has difficulty falling asleep sometimes. What is something that you can do to help yourself relax at bedtime?

Without using words, show what you look like when you are feeling very sad. What helps you feel better when you are feeling sad?

Questions
DARTS

When someone does something that makes you feel very angry, what can you do to stop yourself from losing control?

Sometimes people have memories or flashbacks of frightening things that have happened to them. What is something you could do to cope with a scary memory or flashback?

Thinking of positive thoughts helps us to feel better. What is a positive thought you have?

A hug can feel comforting when we are upset. Who is someone you like to get a hug from?

It is important to spend time doing fun things. What is something you enjoy doing?

What is something that really stresses you out? How can you handle this stress?

Doing a physical activity is a good way to cope with stress. What is a physical activity that you enjoy?

When someone says something that upsets you, what can you say to yourself to keep from losing your cool?

What are some warning signs in your body that let you know you are getting angry? What might help to calm you down?

Focusing on your achievements can help you feel good about yourself. What is something you have achieved?

COMFORT KIT

Theme: Coping With Feelings
Recommended Age Range: 12-16
Treatment Modality: Individual
Stage of Treatment: Middle

Goals
1. Enable awareness of reasons behind self-harming behavior
2. Replace self-harming behavior with self-soothing strategies

Materials
- "My Comfort Kit" worksheet (included)
- Gift bag
- Decorating supplies
- Pencils or markers
- Comfort kit items

Description
The therapist begins by facilitating a discussion about the ways in which people cope in order to survive. For example, "Many people use coping strategies by doing things that they know are not good for them, like overeating, drinking too much alcohol, or smoking. People continue to do these things even though they know these behaviors aren't the best ways to cope with their problems. They continue this behavior because it is hard to stop, or they may not know of other ways to handle their problems. This is similar to self-harming behavior. People sometimes cut themselves or burn themselves on purpose because this is how they deal with their problems. And even though they know it is not the best way to handle their problems, they continue because it is hard to stop, and they do not know of other ways to cope. This activity will help us better understand the reasons why you hurt yourself, and it will give you some ideas about other ways you can cope."

The client then completes the worksheet, "My Comfort Kit," and selects from the list of coping strategies specific ones to try. Next, present the client with a gift bag, and various "comfort items" with which to fill the bag, such as:

- A paper doll to cut up
- A journal in which to draw or write about the emotional pain
- Soothing music
- Momentos that highlight the client's achievements
- Phone number for the crisis line

The client can decorate the comfort kit using the craft supplies provided or cut out pictures from magazines. Encourage the client to use the comfort kit as a substitute for self-harming. In later sessions, the therapist can check in with the client to see how the comfort kit is helping the client to cope better with stress.

Discussion

This activity can be used with adolescents who engage in self-abusive behavior. The therapist must process this activity carefully and with sensitivity. On the one hand, the therapist does not want to condone the client's self-injurious behavior, but, on the other hand, the therapist must not reinforce the client's sense of guilt or shame by suggesting that the client is bad for intentionally engaging in self-harming behavior. Instead, advise that while the acts of self-harm might have served a function, the client has the control to choose a more adaptive coping style. While this activity in itself will likely not alleviate the client's self-harming behavior, it can be used as part of a more comprehensive plan to address this problem.

MY COMFORT KIT

Sometimes kids feel so bad they do things to hurt themselves, like cutting or burning themselves. There are different reasons why kids do this. Check off below the reasons why you think you hurt yourself:

___ I hurt myself because it's a way for me to release my pain.

___ I hurt myself because I think I'm bad and I want to punish myself.

___ I hurt myself because it's a way for me to feel alive.

___ I hurt myself because I feel detached from my feelings and it's a way for me to feel something.

___ I hurt myself because it's a way to get attention.

___ I hurt myself because it's a way for me to let people know I'm in pain and need help.

I hurt myself because _____

If you are committed to getting help for yourself, and finding other ways to cope with your feelings, here are some ideas that other kids have found helpful:

1. Instead of hurting myself to release my pain, I can draw or write about my hurt.

2. Instead of hurting myself to punish myself, I can hit or cut up a doll.

3. Instead of hurting myself to feel alive, I can take my pulse and know that I'm okay.

4. Instead of hurting myself to feel something, I can watch a sad movie or listen to music that moves me.

5. Instead of hurting myself to get attention, I can look at my award to remind myself I can get attention in positive ways.

6. Instead of hurting myself to get help for my pain, I can call the crisis line and talk about my problems.

7. Instead of hurting myself, I can _____

CHAPTER FOUR
SOCIAL SKILLS

Many troubled children and youth are socially immature and antisocial. They lack basic social skills, and as a result, they are often alienated from their peers. Learning to relate appropriately to others, therefore, is an important treatment goal for many children referred for counseling. The socialization games and activities in this chapter can be incorporated into a social skills curriculum, to help children master a variety of social behaviors, such as forming and maintaining healthy friendships, communicating effectively, cooperating with others, maintaining appropriate personal boundaries, and being assertive. As would be expected, socialization activities are most appropriate for use in group counseling settings, so children can learn, practice and rehearse prosocial behaviors. The therapist can observe the group dynamics and provide constructive feedback to children on how they relate to others. Children can also gain insight into their behavior by accepting feedback from their peers.

In choosing a particular activity within this chapter for use in a group setting, the practitioner should consider the stage of group development. Activities that require greater risk taking, or that focus on the enhancement of more advanced social skills, such as "Hugs" and "Nerds, Runts & Dweebs," should be used in later stages of group development. It is also recommended that the therapist join the group in play, in order to model positive social behavior.

MAGIC CARPET RIDE

Theme: Social Skills
Recommended Age Range: 4-7
Treatment Modality: Group
Stage of Treatment: Middle

Goals
1. Strengthen social skills
2. Enhance group cohesion

Materials
• Small carpet or towel large enough for all group members to sit on
• Magic carpet ride stamp book   (included)
• Rubber stamp kit with ink
• 1 puzzle
• 1 jar of bubbles
• 1 plastic tea set
• Juice and cookies

Advance Preparation
Make a booklet for each group member by photocopying the Magic carpet ride stamp book sheet, cutting out the four squares, and then stapling the four pages together in the following order:
1. Sharing
2. Waiting your turn
3. Helping each other
4. Being polite

Description
The group leader enthusiastically tells the children they are going on a magic carpet ride! The leader states that this is a very special journey, and that they will be making four stops. Provide each child with a booklet, and tell them that at each stop, there is a task they need to complete. Once the task is completed, they will get a stamp in their booklet.

Everyone in the group sits on the magic carpet before setting off on their journey (the leader should be theatrical and make various comments to help the children make believe they are truly going on a magic carpet ride!)

At the first stop, "The Land of Sharing," the children must color a picture, using the crayons and paper provided. The children must share the crayons, making sure that each group member gets to use each of the crayons for their picture. Once the task is completed, the leader stamps the first page of each child's booklet. The group then piles onto the magic carpet, and they set off again.

The second stop is "The Land of Waiting Your Turn." Here, the leader passes the bubbles around the group and each child has a turn to blow bubbles. Once all the children have demonstrated the ability to wait their turn for the bubbles, they get the second page of their booklet stamped.

The group sits on the carpet again, and they set off for the third stop, "The Land of Working Together." Here the group must work cooperatively to put the puzzle together. If the group is not working cooperatively, the leader takes the puzzle apart, and has them start over again. The leader can offer suggestions to facilitate group cooperation. Once the puzzle is completed, the leader stamps the third page of each child's booklet.

The group then travels to the final destination, "The Land of Being Polite." The group has a tea party using the plastic tea set, juice and cookies. The leader tells the children they must politely say, "Hello, how are you?" "Please pass the cookies," and "Thank you for the tea." Once the tea party is over, the leader stamps the last page of the booklets, and the group makes its return journey.

Once the children are "home," the group discusses what was learned at each stop on the magic carpet ride.

Discussion
Many children have poorly developed social skills. They have difficulty forming and maintaining friendships, and they set themselves up to be scapegoated by their peers. This activity uses imaginative play to help young children strengthen their interpersonal skills. Children will enjoy the magic carpet ride and the journey to the various "lands." Awarding stamps for appropriate social interaction reinforces their positive behavior. The therapist can make this activity more appealing by incorporating props, costumes, and music for the magic carpet ride.

Magic Carpet Ride Stamp Book

1. **Sharing**	**2.** **Waiting your turn**
3. **Helping each other**	**4.** **Being Polite**

YAK BAK

Theme: Social Skills
Recommended Age Range: 4-12
Treatment Modality: Individual, Group
Stage of Treatment: Middle

Goals
1. Strengthen social skills
2. Enhance communication skills
3. Teach assertiveness skills

Materials
• YAK BAK (Registered Trademark of YES! Entertainment Corporation, 3875 Hopyard Road, Pleasanton, CA 94588. 1-800-222-9376. All Rights Reserved. Used with permission.) (**Note:** A regular tape recorder can be used, but the YAKBAK electronic micro recorder is more engaging.)
• 1 die
• "Practice" and "Funny Noise" cards (included)
• Index cards
• Communication Guide (included)
• Poker chips
• Prizes

Advance Preparation
Copy the Communication Guide onto a large sheet of paper and tape it to the wall so group members can see it.

Divide the index cards into two piles, one for "practice" cards, the other for "funny noise" cards. Select from the list of practice cards that are included those that are appropriate to the age and treatment needs of the children in the group, and copy each onto a separate index card. Write "Practice Card" on the other side of each index card. Use the second pile of index cards for the "Funny Noise" cards. Copy each "Funny Noise" from the list provided onto a separate index card, and write "Funny Noise" onto the other side of these cards.

Description
The activity begins by providing a brief overview of communication skills as follows:

1. The leader gives an example of a "You message," such as, "You took my toy without asking. You have to give it back." "You messages" place blame on the other person. It is more appropriate and effective to use an "I message," such as "I feel angry when you take my toy without asking. I would prefer if you would ask my permission first."

2. The leader summarizes passive, aggressive and assertive communication styles by giving the following example: "If someone takes your toy without asking, a passive response would be to say nothing and pout, a passive-aggressive response would be to say nothing and give that person a mean look, an aggressive response would be to hit that person, and an assertive response would be to say politely, 'That toy belongs to me, so I would appreciate if you would ask my permission if you would like to borrow it'. There's a way you can stand up for yourself without being too mean or pushy."

3. The leader explains the concept of "active listening" by stating: "In order for two people to enjoy being together, they need to be able to listen to each other. When one person is talking, the other person is listening, without interrupting or thinking about something else."

Several examples of the above communication skills can be given, and the children can be asked to volunteer their own examples, to make sure they understand the concepts.

Once the group members understand the basic communication skills, introduce the YAK BAK game as follows:

Players take turns rolling the die. If a player rolls an even number, he draws a "practice" card and reads it aloud to the other player(s). (If this game is being played with younger children, the therapist can read the cards.) The player must practice the given scenario by talking into the YAK BAK. The player then listens to what he has recorded, and has one opportunity to re-record what he wants to say. If desired, a player can ask the therapist or the rest of the group for help or coaching. The other group members can give compliments and clap when the player has successfully completed his turn. If a player rolls an odd number, he draws a "funny noise" card and must make the instructed noise into the YAK BAK. The other players then must try and guess the "funny noise." The game continues until all the players have had a turn.

To encourage positive behavior, the group leader can reward players with tokens throughout the game when players exhibit appropriate social behavior. The tokens can be traded in at the end of the game for a prize.

Variation for younger children: This activity can be simplified for use with younger children to enhance their listening skills. Divide the group into pairs and have each person take turns recording a statement into the YAK BAK while the other listens before repeating what was recorded. The recorded statements should be brief, such as, "My favorite food is ice cream with hot fudge sauce." For added enjoyment, the children can record sound effects!

Discussion
This activity provides children with an opportunity to strengthen their social skills, using the YAK BAK as an engaging tool. Through this game format, children learn how to be better listeners, resolve conflict, make conversation, be polite, and act assertively. Rules can be set at the beginning of the activity, such as, "Only one person records into the YAK BAK at a time, while the others are listening" and "If anyone makes fun of another person, he will lose his turn."

During the activity, the therapist can take advantage of teachable moments by intervening when children act inappropriately. For example, if the children are getting too silly, the therapist can say, "Things are getting out of hand. Nobody likes to be around someone who is acting too silly, so let's settle down." Or if the children are fighting over the use of the YAK BAK, the therapist can say, "Remember that we are supposed to be working on how to share and play nicely with others. What does each person need to change about how they're acting right now?" It can also help to assign one of the quieter group members the role of "rule monitor" to assist the group in following the rules set out at the beginning.

At the end of the activity, the therapist can ask the group for examples of how they can apply the skills learned in this session to situations outside the therapy setting.

Practice Cards
YAK BAK

Your aunt gave you a present for your birthday. Practice thanking her for the gift.

You are playing in the sandbox at the park. Practice asking another child if you can borrow his shovel.

Your sister lent you her toy, and you accidentally broke it. Practice apologizing to her.

You have a friend over. Practice offering him some candy that you have left over from a party you went to.

You are playing a new game on the computer, and you don't understand the instructions. Practice asking an adult for help.

You do poorly on a test at school. The other children in the class tease you and call you "stupid." Practice how you would deal with this in words, rather than getting into a fight.

You are invited to a birthday party. You don't know any of the other children at the party. Practice going up to someone you don't know, introducing yourself, and making conversation for one minute.

There is a child in your class that you have become friendly with. Your parents have given you permission to have him over to your house to play. Practice inviting him over.

You are at the movies, and you are in line to buy popcorn. Another person pushes in front of you. Practice what you would say to that person, without getting into a fight.

You had plans to get together with a friend. Your friend calls you at the last minute to cancel. Later you find out that your friend got together with someone else, instead of you. Practice talking to your friend about this.

Make up a situation in which someone is asking for something in a rude way, then practice saying the same thing but in a polite way.

You and a friend are going to play a game she has never played before. First explain the game in a bossy way, and then practice explaining the game in a helpful way.

Funny Noise Cards
YAK BAK

cow	train
cat	siren
dog	bell
rooster	clock
duck	car
bee	popcorn popping
birds chirping	someone snoring
the wind howling	someone slurping soup

Communication Guide

Do's	Don'ts
Listen	Interrupt
Concentrate on what the person is saying	Blame
Look the person in the eye	Act bossy
Use "I messages"	Raise your voice or yell
Stand up for yourself without being rude	Make fun of the other person

HUGS

Theme: Social Skills
Recommended Age Range: 4-12
Treatment Modality: Group, Family
Stage of Treatment: Middle

Goals
1. Promote positive social behavior
2. Teach the concept of boundaries and personal space
3. Facilitate assertive behavior

Materials
- Teddy bear stickers
- Gift box
- Message labels (included)
- 4 sheets each of two different colors of tissue paper
- Adhesive labels
- Tape

Advance Preparation
Copy each message from the list provided onto a separate adhesive label.

Place the teddy bear stickers in a gift box. Wrap the box in layers of tissue paper, one layer for each player. Attach an instruction label from the list included to each layer. The innermost label will read: "Everyone in this group has done a great job learning about hugs and safe touching. Open this gift and share it with the group. Take the teddy bear stickers home, as a reminder that you can ask for a BEAR HUG when you need a hug from someone you care about!"

Description
The group members sit in a circle. Holding up the tissue-wrapped package, the leader announces that there is a gift for the group. However, before they can find out what it is, everyone has to take turns unwrapping it, and following the instructions written on each layer. The leader then gives the gift to the person whose birthday comes up next. The person unwraps the first layer. The gift is then passed to the left until it arrives at the last person in the circle, who reads the final message. The teddy bear stickers are distributed to the group members.

Discussion
This is a short but fun activity that can be used at the end of a session focusing on social skills. It provides an interactive approach to learning about safe touching and personal boundaries. Assertiveness skills are enhanced as group members have the opportunity to ask for hugs or decline being touched. This is an important activity both for children whose bodies have been violated, and for children who have difficulty maintaining appropriate personal boundaries. However, some children who have been sexually or physically abused cannot tolerate being touched, and they may become very anxious during this activity. Therefore, this activity should

67

only be used with children who have sufficiently addressed boundary and touch issues in their treatment. Similarly, if this activity is being used with sexually intrusive children, it should only be introduced once all group members have made considerable progress in the area of boundary control. The therapist must be particularly prudent during the activity to ensure that the children feel safe and comfortable, and intervene if necessary.

In addition to being used in children's treatment groups, this activity is also appropriate for family sessions. The family therapist can facilitate the activity by stressing the importance of personal privacy and rules about touching. The activity can also be used to help parents learn how to physically nurture their children by offering hugs at appropriate times.

Message Labels
HUGS

Everyone in this group has done a great job learning about hugs and safe touching. Open this gift and share it with the group. Take the teddy bear stickers home, as a reminder that you can ask for a BEAR HUG when you need a hug from someone you care about!

We all need a hug once in a while. Ask someone in the group for a hug.

It's okay to say "NO" if you don't want to be touched. Practice saying, "I don't want to be touched right now."

You can make yourself feel good by hugging yourself! Practice giving yourself a hug.

Sometimes we don't like it when other people come too close to us. Practice standing an arm's length away from another person in this group.

A hug can feel great as long as you aren't hugged too hard. Practice giving someone in the group a hug without hugging that person too hard. Don't forget to ask that person's permission before you give a hug!

Hugs can feel great as long as you don't touch someone on their private body parts. Practice giving someone in the group a hug without touching them on their private body parts. Don't forget to ask the person's permission before you give a hug!

Hugs are for people we know and trust. We don't hug strangers, like people we never met at the grocery store! Practice giving a hug to someone in the group you know and trust. Don't forget to ask that person's permission before you give a hug!

It's time for a group hug! Have everyone in the group stand in a close circle and give a group hug. Remember, you don't have to join a group hug if you don't want to.

BUILDING BLOCKS

Theme: Social Skills
Recommended Age Range: 7-16
Treatment Modality: Group, Family
Stage of Treatment: Middle

Goals
1. Promote positive social behavior
2. Encourage group cooperation
3. Strengthen group cohesion

Materials
• An assortment of wooden or plastic building blocks
• Flip chart paper
• Tape
• 2 Worksheets per group member (included)

Advance Preparation
Copy the following rules onto one sheet of flip chart paper:
1. Everyone has a turn
2. Everyone reacts politely to all ideas
3. Everyone gives a compliment when someone finishes a turn
4. Everyone treats the building blocks with care

Description
The group sits in a circle, and one group member is chosen to be the observer. The leader dumps the building blocks into the middle of the circle, and instructs the group to build something with the blocks. The leader states that the group has to build something using all of the blocks, in only two minutes. During the building time, the observer watches the interaction. At the end of the two minutes, the leader asks the observer and the group to discuss the group process, using the following questions as a guide for the discussion (these questions can be adapted, depending on the age of the group members).

Did everyone participate equally, or did some people choose not to share the blocks?
How did people in the group treat the blocks?
How did each person feel during the building process?
What kind of atmosphere was created in the group (cooperative or uncooperative)?

Next, the group leader tapes the rules to the wall so that each person in the group can see them. The rules are reviewed to ensure that all the group members understand them. The group is asked to once again build something using all of the blocks in two minutes, but this time, following the rules on the flip chart paper. At the end of the two minutes, the leader poses the same questions as above and the observer and the group discuss the difference between the two group building processes. Additional questions can be asked to further emphasize the value of positive group interaction, such as:

What did you learn today about working together?
What do you think would have happened if one person did not want to cooperate?
How do you think learning to cooperate will help you at home and at school?

Discussion

This exercise facilitates the development of interpersonal skills. If this activity is being used with children who have limited group-processing skills, it may be helpful to videotape the group, then have the children comment on what they observe. Or, have the group members complete the worksheet with the discussion questions and then discuss their responses to each of the questions. This way, each group member has the opportunity to think about the group process before he shares his responses with the group.

BUILDING BLOCKS DISCUSSION QUESTIONS

1. Did everyone participate equally, or did some people choose not to share the blocks?

_____

_____

2. How did people in the group treat the blocks?

_____

_____

3. How did you feel during the building activity? (Good, bad, respected, left out)

_____

_____

4. What kind of atmosphere was created in the group? (cooperative or uncooperative)

_____

_____

NERDS, RUNTS, AND DWEEBS

Theme: Social Skills
Recommended Age Range: 7-16
Treatment Modality: Group
Stage of Treatment: Middle

Goals
1. Promote positive social behavior
2. Disarm negative feelings brought on by teasing from peers
3. Encourage group cooperation
4. Strengthen group cohesion

Materials
• NERDS ®, RUNTS ®, and DWEEBS ® candy (Trademarks of Société des Produits Nestlé SA. Vevey, Switzerland. All Rights Reserved. Used with permission.)
• Index cards
• Paper, scissors, and tape to make team arm bands or head bands (optional)
• Score sheet (included)

Advance Preparation
Copy each scenario below onto a separate index card:

NERDS: You are invited to a cousin's party, and you do not know most of the children there. You are very shy, but you decide to take a risk and meet someone new. Role-play how you would approach another person at the party and make conversation.

RUNTS: You are walking home from school and you decide to stop at the corner store to buy a chocolate bar. At the store, you bump into a group of kids from your school. One of the kids is a bully, and he demands that you give him all of your money. Role-play how you could appropriately stand up for yourself in this situation.

DWEEBS: Kids at school are teasing you again, calling you names like "loser" and "stupid." Usually, you would handle this by getting into a fight and punching the person who is teasing you. However, you have been attending a social skills group, and have learned some appropriate verbal responses to this kind of teasing. Role-play how you would handle this situation.

Description
The group is divided into three teams: NERDS, RUNTS, or DWEEBS. Each team is provided with an index card that has one of the above scenarios written on it. Each team must create a skit to put on for the rest of the group. The skits must have a beginning, middle and end. One person on each team will be the director of the skit, one person will write down the interaction of the team as they are preparing for the skit, and the rest of the team will be involved in the skit. The group leader will complete the score sheet. In addition to preparing and rehearsing a

skit, each team will come up with a team cheer and logo for headbands or armbands. The skits are performed in front of the rest of the group, and additional points are awarded to teams who watch quietly as the skits are being performed, and who clap enthusiastically at the end of each skit. NERDS, RUNTS, and DWEEBS candy are awarded at the end of each skit as prizes.

Variation: If the three kinds of candy cannot be found, just use NERDS candy, which are readily available at candy stores, and have each group make up a "NERD" cheer and team logo.

Discussion

Group therapy is an ideal setting in which to help children modify and enhance their social skills. Through the preparation, rehearsal and performance of skits, group members are provided with the opportunity to learn how to interact with others in a more positive manner. The group leader can further enhance the learning process by taking advantage of teachable moments as situations arise during the session. For example, if group members are acting inappropriately, the leader can stop the activity and state, "I am noticing that people in the group are not treating others with respect. What does each person in the group need to do differently right now, to be more respectful?" There are many opportunities for the group leader to provide the group members with positive feedback when they exhibit appropriate behavior.

Additional learning can occur through a group discussion following the skits. The group leader can pose several questions for the group to discuss, for example, "What did you learn today about working together? What can be learned from the skits about relating to other people? And, how can you use the skills learned in this activity to help you get along better with others?"

In addition to enhancing social skills, this activity also deals with the theme of being a social outcast. Children who lack social skills are often ruthlessly teased by other children, which leads to negative feelings and a poor self-image. However, this activity encourages group members to celebrate being a nerd, runt or dweeb in order to counter and alleviate negative feelings children experience when their peers torment them.

SCORE SHEET

POINTS	NERDS	RUNTS	DWEEBS
Everyone on the team participates			
Everyone on the team cooperates			
Everyone listens attentively to others			
The team shows enthusiasm			
Nobody acts too silly			
The skit has a beginning, middle and end			

FRIENDSHIP BRACELETS

Theme: Social Skills
Recommended Age Range: 9 -16
Treatment Modality: Group
Stage of Treatment: Beginning, Middle

Goals

1. Facilitate formation of healthy friendships
2. Encourage awareness of what traits are valued in friendships
3. Enhance group cohesion

Materials

• "Friends" worksheet (included)
• Friendship bracelets

Advance Preparation

Copy enough worksheets for each person in the group.

Description

Group members complete the worksheet, "Friends," then share their responses with the group. The leader can facilitate further discussion about how to form friendships, respond to peer pressure, and resolve conflict. The children can discuss how an atmosphere of safety and acceptance can be created in the group. Next, the leader can affirm the cohesion of the group by distributing friendship bracelets to all of the group members. As an alternative, the group can make their own friendship bracelets.

Discussion

This group experience is designed to enhance pro-social behavior by helping children learn the specific skills needed to form and maintain healthy friendships. The experiential opportunity provided in the group setting allows children to practice and strengthen social skills in a safe and supportive environment. The friendship bracelets are used to affirm the children's sense of belonging and acceptance in the group. Ultimately, strengthening the children's social skills will have a positive influence on their development.

FRIENDS

1. If you could design the perfect friend, what would that person be like? Write down the qualities you look for in a friend in the space provided below. Put a star next to the qualities that you possess.

_____

_____

_____

_____

2. What do kids do in order to become popular and fit in with others? Give some examples of when you have felt pressured to do something in order to fit in.

_____

_____

_____

_____

_____

3. What are some ways to make and keep a friend? Write your ideas down in the space provided below.

_____

_____

_____

_____

_____

4. Sometimes people have arguments with their friends. Give an example of when this has happened to you. Write down some ideas of how you can deal with this kind of conflict.

_____

_____

_____

_____

_____

CHAPTER FIVE
SELF-ESTEEM

Most troubled children and youth suffer from a damaged sense of self. Some children have such profound self-esteem issues that they have internalized the belief that they are "bad" and their future is hopeless. The goal of enhancing self-esteem for these troubled children is not an easy one, yet it is an essential component of any successful treatment program. In order to help children achieve this important treatment goal, various activities from this chapter can be implemented. These activities can be used as tools to help children focus on their strengths and abilities, promote feelings of self-worth, encourage a more optimistic attitude, and instill a message of hope for the future.

In order to be truly effective at strengthening a child's self-esteem, caregivers must be part of the process. Many caregivers need to be taught and coached how to interact with their children in a positive way, and how to foster their children's unique talents. The activities in this chapter are, therefore, greatly enhanced by working in conjunction with caregivers.

KING OR QUEEN FOR THE DAY

Theme: Self-esteem
Recommended Age Range: 4-10
Treatment Modality: Group, Family
Stage of Treatment: Middle

Goals

1. Enhance self-esteem
2. Facilitate internalization of positive messages

Materials

• Gold or yellow cardboard
• A robe
• Decorating supplies, such as markers, glitter and stickers
• Tape
• Chair

Advance Preparation

Decorate a chair to make it look like a throne.

Description

The leader explains that this session is a very special one, as the children are going to be treated like kings or queens. First, the children construct and decorate their cardboard crowns, and then they take turns dressing up in a crown and robe. One at a time, each child sits on the "throne" while the rest of the group lavishes praise. As each child dismounts the "throne", the rest of the group bows to the child. The group can then have a festive celebration with "royal music" and a special snack.

Discussion

Helping children to feel special, worthy, and valued is a tremendously powerful therapeutic intervention. Enhancing children's self-esteem is a major component of their healing process, and it fosters their resilience. Children will be captivated by this activity as they revel in their moment of being treated like royalty! Ultimately, it is hoped that the children will integrate the messages of praise so they can establish a more positive sense of self.

SMILEY FACES

Theme: Self-esteem
Recommended Age Range: 7-12
Treatment Modality: Individual, Group, Family
Stage of Treatment: Middle

Goals
1. Encourage positive and optimistic attitudes
2. Help promote self worth

Materials
• "Smiley Faces" game (included)
• 2 quarters
• Gift bag filled with inexpensive items, preferably with the happy face logo
• Bright yellow cardboard or poster board
• Black marker
• Markers or pens
• Tape

Advance Preparation
Photocopy and enlarge the "Smiley Faces" game. If possible, laminate it onto cardboard for greater durability.

Cut out circles the size of a paper plate, one for each person in the group including the leader and adult helpers. Use a black marker to draw a happy face on each circle.

Description
The therapist begins the activity by pointing out that people generally feel happier if they have a positive attitude, focus on happy thoughts, and do things that make them feel good. The therapist explains that the purpose of this activity is to help each person develop a more positive attitude, so that he can feel better.

Group members sit in a circle with the game board and coin placed in the middle of the circle. This coin is the game marker. The game is explained as follows:

Players take turns flipping the coin. Heads means advance to the next space on the board, tails means lose a turn. At each new space, answer the question provided. If the space has a happy face, distribute items from the gift bag to everyone in the group. Play until the coin reaches the end of the path.

For a closing activity, tape the pre-cut cardboard happy faces to the backs of each group member and the leader, and have the children and the leader write something nice on everyone's happy face. This is a nice momento for each person to take home at the end of the session.

Discussion

The notion of cognitive behavior therapy is to help people learn to change the way they think, behave, and feel. The "Smiley Faces" game helps children internalize positive thoughts, which, in turn, will lead to enhanced self-esteem. This is an empowering activity as it helps children realize that they have the power to change how they feel by focusing on positive things.

Although this activity facilitates a focus on positive feelings, there are times when negative feelings are healthy and appropriate. Therefore, within the context of this activity, the therapist should reinforce the message that while it is important to have an optimistic attitude, it is normal and acceptable for people to experience both positive and negative feelings.

SMILEY FACES GAME

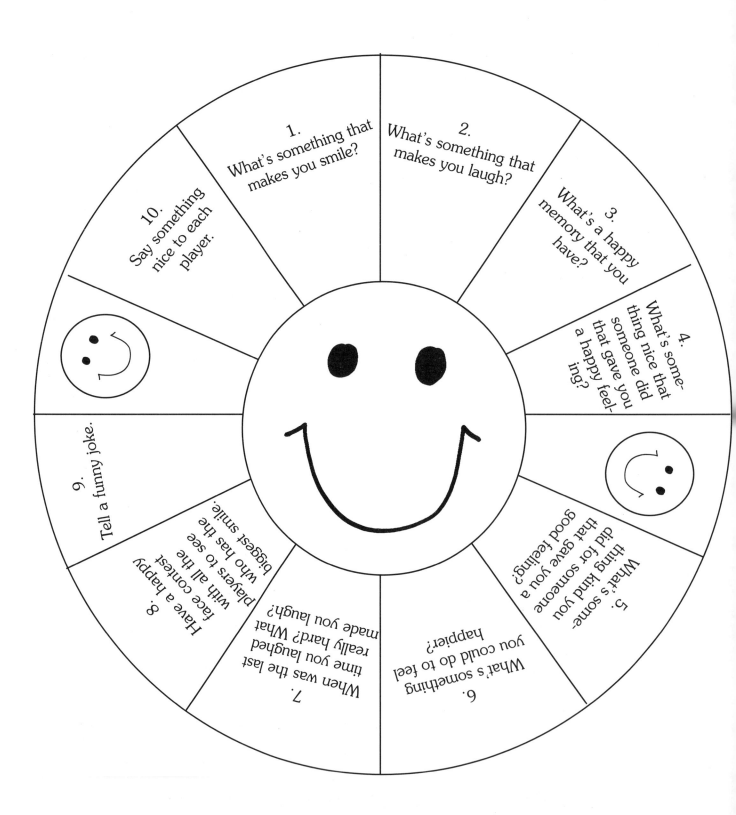

1. What's something that makes you smile?

2. What's something that makes you laugh?

3. What's a happy memory that you have?

4. What's something nice that someone did that gave you a happy feeling?

5. What's something kind you did for someone that gave you a good feeling?

6. What's something you could do to feel happier?

7. When was the last time you laughed really hard? What made you laugh?

8. Have a happy face contest with all the players to see who has the biggest smile.

9. Tell a funny joke.

10. Say something nice to each player.

CELEBRATION

Theme: Self-esteem
Recommended Age Range: 7-16
Treatment Modality: Group, Family
Stage of Treatment: Middle, End

Goals

1. Enhance self-esteem
2. Facilitate internalization of positive messages

Materials

- "Celebration" worksheet (included)
- Assortment of party decorations
- Party hats
- Loot bags
- Six gift bags
- Six gift tags
- Noisemakers or party horns
- Balloons
- Temporary teddy bear tattoos
- Glitter stars
- Happy face stickers
- Pompom or cotton balls for use as warm fuzzies
- Die
- Party music (optional)

Advance Preparation

Copy a worksheet for each child. Fill and label six gift bags as follows:

1. Fill a gift bag with blow horns and attach a gift tag with the following message: "Blow your own horn to show how proud you are of yourself!"
2. Fill a gift bag with balloons and attach a gift tag with the following message: "Take a balloon to celebrate the pleasures of life!"
3. Fill a gift bag with happy face stickers and attach a gift tag with the following message: "Have a happy face sticker to celebrate laughter!"
4. Fill a gift bag with teddy bear tattoos and attach a gift tag with the following message: "Wear a teddy bear tattoo as a reminder that you can ask for a bear hug from the people who care about you!"
5. Fill a gift bag with glitter stars and attach a gift tag with the following message: "Help yourself to a glitter star as a reminder that you are a shining star!"
6. Fill a gift bag with pompom balls (or cotton balls) and attach a gift tag with the following message: "Have a warm fuzzy to show you can help yourself feel good!"

Description

Group members complete their "Celebration" worksheets (instead of writing their responses, younger children can draw pictures.) When all members have filled in their worksheets, the therapist leads a discussion about the importance of celebrating and honoring the special and unique qualities of the people in the group. The leader explains that the group members are going to celebrate each other by playing a party game.

Group members sit in a circle with their completed worksheets in front of them and the six gift bags in the middle of the circle. The leader distributes party hats and loot bags to each group member, creating a celebratory atmosphere. Group members take turns rolling the die and sharing their responses for the question on the worksheet that matches the number on the die. For example, if a player rolls three, that player shares his response for box three on the worksheet ("Something that makes me laugh"). All players then share their answers in box three. At the end of each question, award a party favor. (**Note:** Each question corresponds to a particular party favor, as the gifts and message tags are related to the questions on the worksheet.)

The game is played until all six numbers of the die have been rolled and each of the six questions on the worksheet has been answered. If during the game, a player rolls a number that has already been used, the player rolls again until a new number comes up. When all the questions have been answered and the loot bags have been filled with party favors, party music can be played and the group can dance to the music!

Discussion

More often than not, therapy focuses on client problems. This activity, however, directs attention to what is good in the child's life. Therapeutically, this is very helpful, as it enables children to think positively. This activity demonstrates that one does not need a special event to have a celebration. Celebrations can occur every day, to celebrate even the small joys in life, and to applaud one's efforts and accomplishments.

CELEBRATION WORKSHEET

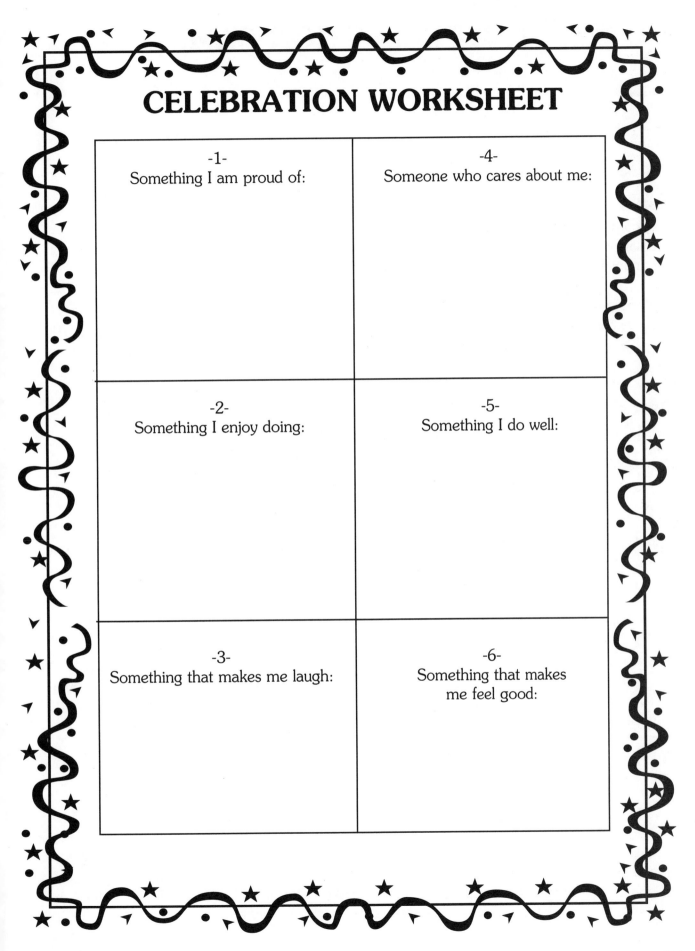

-1- Something I am proud of:	-4- Someone who cares about me:
-2- Something I enjoy doing:	-5- Something I do well:
-3- Something that makes me laugh:	-6- Something that makes me feel good:

THE PERFECTION GAME

Theme: Self-esteem
Recommended Age Range: 7-16
Treatment Modality: Individual
Stage of Treatment: Middle

Goals
1. Encourage use of positive self-talk
2. Disarm negative self-talk
3. Enhance self-esteem

Materials
• The PERFECTION game (PERFECTION ® is a Trademark of Hasbro. © 1999 Hasbro. All Rights Reserved. Used with permission.)
• Paper and craft supplies

Description
Explain the concept of self-talk by stating, "Most people carry on silent conversations with themselves; this is called self-talk. We tend to repeat the same messages to ourselves over and over, and soon, we come to believe these silent messages. For example, if I were to repeat 'I cannot do anything right,' I would soon believe this. I would feel badly, and then I would probably not do as well."

Next, the therapist and child make a list of negative self-talk statements by taking turns. Some things to include:
I'm so stupid.
I can't do anything right.
There's no point in even trying.

The therapist and child then start to play the PERFECTION game. First, move the timer to the ON position, press down the pop-up tray, and have the child quickly try to fit the plastic shapes into the matching holes on the tray while repeating negative self-talk statements. Once the first round is completed, the therapist and child make a list of positive self-talk statements. For example:
Nobody is perfect.
I can try my best.
I will do better if I relax.

The child plays a second round of the PERFECTION game, but this time, repeating the positive self-talk statements while playing the game. The therapist and child then discuss the difference in how it felt to play the two rounds, first making discouraging self-talk statements and then making encouraging self-talk statements. The therapist reinforces the concept that positive self-talk helps people feel better about themselves and perform better.

As a closing activity, the child can compile the positive self-talk statements into a book and then decorate it.

Discussion

Most clients make negative, irrational and self-defeating statements about themselves which often lead to heightened feelings of worthlessness and anxiety. It is important to help clients replace negative, self-defeating statements with positive, self-enhancing statements. Self-talk is a skill children can use when they are feeling discouraged, angry, anxious or afraid. Children can be prompted to rehearse and memorize self-talk statements, so that they have a repertoire to use when they are feeling upset or overwhelmed.

OVER THE RAINBOW

Theme: Self-esteem
Recommended Age Range: 7-16
Treatment Modality: Individual, Group, Family
Stage of Treatment: Middle, End

Goals

1. Provide a message of hope for the future
2. Instill the belief that people can pursue their hopes and dreams

Materials

- Four pieces of letter-size paper (or larger), each a different color
- Tape
- Small brass pot
- Chocolate gold coins
- Gift tag

Advance Preparation

Fill a small brass pot with chocolate gold coins to create a pot of gold. Write the following message on the gift tag: "You can reach the pot of gold at the end of the rainbow if you follow your dreams, believe in yourself, think positive thoughts, and never give up hope!" Attach the gift tag to the pot of gold.

Copy each question from the list below onto separate pieces of paper:
1. You can reach the pot of gold at the end of the rainbow if you follow your dreams! What is your dream and how are you working towards it?
2. You can reach the pot of gold at the end of the rainbow if you believe in yourself! What is something positive that you believe about yourself?
3. You can reach the pot of gold at the end of the rainbow if you think positive! What positive thoughts do you have?
4. You can reach the pot of gold at the end of the rainbow if you never give up hope! What hopes do you have for your future?

Spread the four pieces of paper on the floor in an arch shape, like a rainbow. Place the pot of gold at the end of the paper arch.

Description

The activity begins by discussing dreams, hopes, and wishes for the future. The therapist explains the activity to the child as follows:

Stand on the first colored square at the beginning of the arch, read the question aloud, and answer the question. (If desired, the therapist can participate along with the client.) Step to the next colored square and answer the second question. Proceed in the same manner to the third and fourth squares. Once you reach the pot of gold at the end of the rainbow, read the message on the gift tag and help yourself to the treat!

Discussion

Instilling a sense of hope for the future is an important component of treatment. This activity takes on added therapeutic importance with clients who feel discouraged or hopeless, as the activity helps them to see that things can get better. The activity empowers, as it communicates the message that people can create a better future for themselves if they remain positive and persevere.

THE HERO IN YOU

Theme: Self-esteem
Recommended Age Range: 9-16
Treatment Modality: Individual, Group, Family
Stage of Treatment: Middle, End

Goals

1. Enhance self-esteem
2. Instill the message that people are resilient
3. Provide a message of hope for the future

Materials

• Song: "Hero" © by Mariah Carey (Copyright by Sony Music)
• Tape deck or compact disc player
• Paper and coloring supplies

Description

Play Mariah Carey's song, "Hero" and ask the children to close their eyes, listen carefully to the words, and think about the messages in the song. After the song has finished, have the children write or draw images or thoughts on how the song made them feel. Children can then share their work, and discuss the messages in the song.

Discussion

Well-trained therapists understand and appreciate the healing power of music. The song "Hero" and the expressive arts activity that follows is used in the therapeutic context to affect the child's mood, stimulate emotion, and act as a catalyst for improved self-awareness and self-esteem. The theme of the song, that there is a hero within us all, conveys to children that they are strong and resilient.

GRADUATION CEREMONIES

GRADUATION CEREMONIES

When working with troubled children and youth, the therapist must handle the termination phase of treatment with particular sensitivity. Terminating treatment can be seen as a mourning process and as a re-enactment of earlier experiences of loss. During this phase of the intervention process, the child may experience feelings of sadness, anger, rejection and abandonment. Notwithstanding, termination can also be a wonderfully positive experience as the child's progress and achievements in therapy are highlighted and celebrated. Whether a child is ending therapy, finishing a group counseling program, attending the last day at a day-treatment school program, or being discharged from residential treatment, the ending experience should have several key components:

1. The child's feelings about ending treatment should be normalized, validated, and processed with care and sensitivity.
2. The child should be prepared well in advance of the actual termination. The therapist should clearly outline to the child how and when the therapy will end.
3. The child and the child's primary caregivers should be included in the discharge planning.
4. Several sessions during this last phase of intervention should be devoted to helping the child express any ambivalent feelings about ending treatment. Activities should be chosen that help the child to express his feelings, review his progress, and honor his accomplishments. For example, the child can draw a picture of what he thinks it will be like to say good bye to the therapist. Another activity is to have the child make a collage to illustrate how far he has come in treatment.
5. The child's accomplishments in treatment should be documented, so the child has a concrete representation of his therapeutic success, and a lasting record after treatment is terminated.

Graduation ceremonies provide a structure to the termination process, and help create a positive, celebratory atmosphere for this important phase of intervention. The following are some suggested ideas that can be included in the graduation ceremony:

Invitations
The child can choose whom to invite to his graduation ceremony. The child and therapist can together make and decorate the invitations.

Graduation certificate
The child can be presented with a certificate at the graduation ceremony. The certificate provides the child with a lasting record of his achievements (See Appendix A for a sample certificate.)

Loot bag
When a child attends a birthday party, he is often given a loot bag at the end. This provides a means to express gratitude to the child for his participation in the celebration and marks the end of the birthday party. Drawing on this idea,the child can be given a loot bag at his graduation ceremony. The loot bag can be filled with items and a note can be attached to the loot bag that offers a nurturing, hopeful, and affirming therapeutic message. (See Appendix A for a sample loot bag.)

Letter

The therapist, primary worker or member of the program staff can write a letter to present to the child at his graduation ceremony. This letter will review goals achieved in treatment and validate the child's efforts and accomplishments. (See Appendix A for a sample review letter.) The therapist can ask other people who are significant to the child to write letters for presentation to the child at the ceremony.

Speeches

A graduation ceremony is not complete without speeches! The therapist can be the Master of Ceremonies during the party. If they wish, the child and invited guests can give a speech during the ceremony.

Graduation picture

Take a picture of the child (the graduate) for him to take home and add to his collection of memorabilia.

Message wall

Hang a large piece of poster board on the counseling room wall, for each child to sign at the graduation ceremony. The child should only sign his first name, in order to protect confidentiality. If desired, the child can write a "message of hope" to other children who will see it when they attend their counseling sessions.

Cake

As a final closing ritual, present the child with a cake decorated with a congratulatory message.

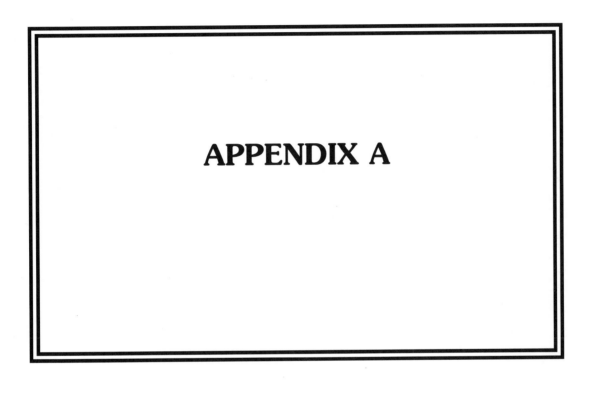

APPENDIX A

Graduation Certificate

_____

(Client's Name)

**This certificate is presented to you
in honor of all the tremendous
progress you have made.
I am very proud of you!**

_____   _____

(Counselor's signature)   (Witness)

_____

(Date)

Sample Letter of Review

Below is a letter of review I wrote to a 10-year-old client whose mother had died of AIDS:

Dear Beth,

I am writing you this letter to let you know how proud I am of you! You have worked so hard over the last year, and you have made wonderful progress.

I remember when you first came to see me. You were very quiet, and it was hard for you to talk about your mom's death. Even though you were so unhappy, you smiled all the time because you didn't want to face the sad feelings that you had inside.

I remember that you started to open up when we did the "Butterflies in my Stomach" activity. You were able to share some of your worries and talk about your mixed-up feelings. The special game of CANDY LAND we played also helped you talk about your feelings. I remember how much you loved to play the game, and how you begged me each session to play it again! Each time we played it, you got better at sharing your feelings, and you also got to eat a lot of jellybeans!

You've come a long way in being able to express yourself. Remember how you used clay to let out your mad feelings? Before you came to see me, you were getting into fights with other kids. Now when you get mad, instead of losing your cool, you are using the ideas that you learned in our sessions, like punching a pillow, counting to ten, and talking to your aunt. That's great progress!

We played many games together, but the TROUBLE game stands out as one of the games that I think really helped you a lot. I remember when we played the game, we talked about how you blamed yourself for your mom's death and how you wished you could have taken care of your mom and saved her. But you were just a little girl, and your mom was too sick. It is very sad that she died, but unfortunately, nobody could have saved her. I'm glad that the TROUBLE game helped you to finally understand that your mom's death was not your fault. And I am glad to hear that you keep the lucky pennies that you got from the TROUBLE game by your bed as a reminder that you are not a bad person and you deserve to have good things happen to you.

Sometimes when you think about your mom, or when something good happens in your life and your mom isn't around to share the occasion, you may feel sad. It is normal and okay to cry and to let the sadness out! And, when you have happy times, it doesn't mean that you have forgotten your mom. I am sure that she would have wanted you to be happy and to enjoy life.

You have already been through a lot in your young life, but your experiences have made you a stronger person. Beth, you are a very special person; you are kind and caring, you are a hard worker, and you have a great sense of humor. You can be the kind of person your mom would be proud of.

A few weeks ago, when we did the "Over the Rainbow" activity, we talked about your hopes and dreams for your future. I think it's really neat that you want to be a veterinarian! No matter what you choose to be, you will succeed if you continue to believe in yourself!

Beth, I have enjoyed working with you. You have done a great job in sorting out your feelings, and in talking about some very hard stuff. I will cherish your graduation picture that now hangs proudly on my wall of fame, and I will remember your wonderfull giggles and your sparkling eyes gazing toward a bright future!.

I wish you all the best,

Liana

Sample Loot bag

I presented the following loot bag to a 14-year-old female adolescent at the time of her graduation from therapy. Feel free to adapt the loot bag to suit your client.

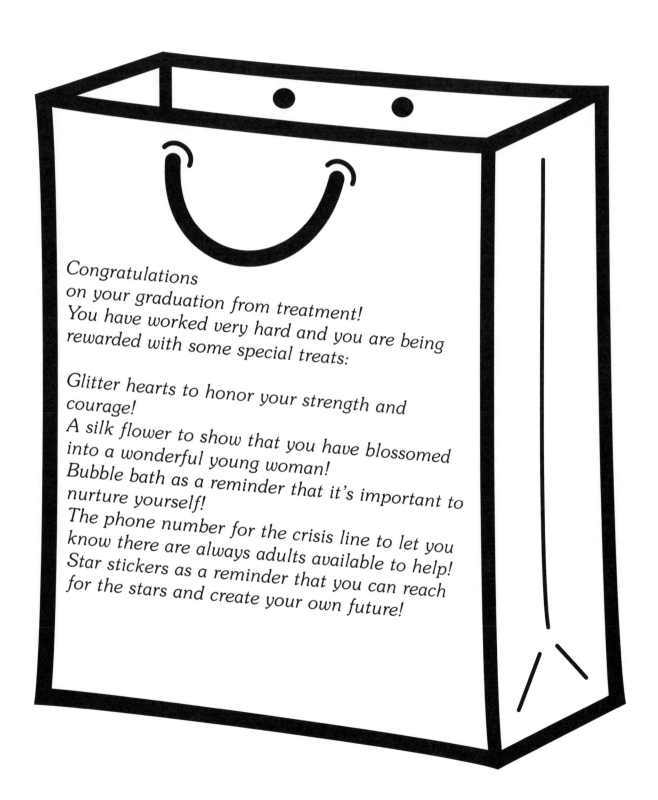

Congratulations
on your graduation from treatment!
You have worked very hard and you are being
rewarded with some special treats:

Glitter hearts to honor your strength and
courage!
A silk flower to show that you have blossomed
into a wonderful young woman!
Bubble bath as a reminder that it's important to
nurture yourself!
The phone number for the crisis line to let you
know there are always adults available to help!
Star stickers as a reminder that you can reach
for the stars and create your own future!

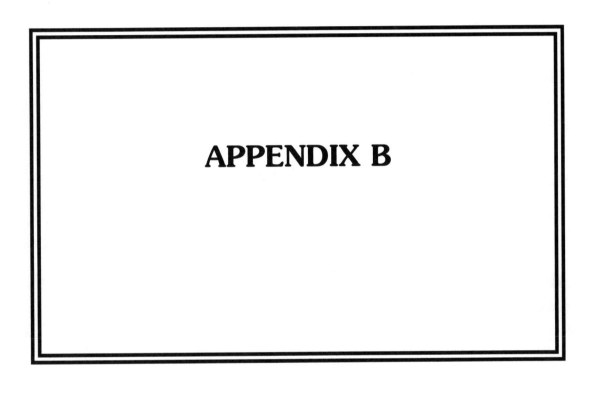

APPENDIX B

CONSULTATION & TRAINING SERVICES PROVIDED BY LIANA LOWENSTEIN

Liana Lowenstein offers clinical consultation and innovative workshops that can be tailored to meet your specific training needs.

Clinical Case Consultation

Mental health professionals and agencies can take advantage of clinical consultation in a number of areas, including child welfare, child sexual abuse, bereaved children, and "hard to serve" cases.

Play Therapy Supervision

Clinical supervision can be arranged face to face or by telephone. Hours can be counted toward play therapy certification or registration.

Consultation on Curriculum Development

For those developing a children's treatment group, this consultation will help create an innovative curriculum. Included is a package containing activities designed specifically for your group program, reproducible worksheets, sample forms, resource lists, and other useful materials.

Consultation on Developing a Child Sexual Abuse Treatment Program

This consultation supports agencies and communities seeking to develop new sexual abuse treatment programs or strengthen existing services. Options for various program models are outlined. As well, it furnishes program descriptions and materials, so that a full range of services can be implemented, including crisis intervention, trauma assessment, and long-term treatment.

Play Therapy Training

Through a dynamic, hands-on learning experience, these workshops - available in half-day, full-day or intensive, multi-day training sessions - impart various play therapy techniques for use with a broad variety of client populations. They're available in a number of topics, including:

- Creative Interventions for Troubled Children and Youth
- Assessing and Treating Sexually Traumatized Children
- Therapeutic Scrapbooks With Traumatized Children
- Play Therapy Techniques for Bereaved Children
- Innovative Play Therapy Approaches for Children and Youth With ADHD

For further information, please contact:
Liana Lowenstein, Pharma Plus, PO Box 91012,
2901 Bayview Avenue, Toronto, Ontario, Canada M2K 1H0
(E-mail) liana@globalserve.net

Innovative Child Therapy Books

Creative Interventions for Troubled Children & Youth

By Liana Lowenstein

This best-selling collection features creative assessment and treatment activities designed to engage resistant clients in counseling. Activities are outlined to help preschool, latency, and adolescent clients address issues such as feelings identification, coping strategies, social skills, and self-esteem, and there is a special section on termination activities. *Creative Interventions* is replete with practical tools to help make individual, group, and family therapy sessions meaningful and effective.

More Creative Interventions for Troubled Children & Youth

By Liana Lowenstein

Liana Lowenstein's exciting new book presents more creative interventions to engage, assess, and treat children, youth, and families. Games, art, music, role-plays, and stories are used to help reach resistant clients and enable them to identify and express feelings, manage anger, develop social skills, and enhance self-esteem. This book also includes a special section on managing challenging client behavior. *More Creative Interventions* is an essential resource for practitioners seeking to add new and innovative counseling activities to their repertory.

Paper Dolls and Paper Airplanes:
Therapeutic Exercises for Sexually Traumatized Children

By Geraldine Crisci, Marilynn Lay, and Liana Lowenstein

This hands-on treatment manual is brimming with more than 80 innovative activities for individual or group therapy sessions with sexually abused children of all ages. Creative, engaging exercises are used to lower the threat level of therapy and help clients to address treatment issues such as feelings, disclosure, self-blame, offenders, triggers, sexuality, safety, and self-esteem. This best-selling book is an invaluable tool for practitioners working with sexually abused children.

- -

Order Form

Name: _____ Agency: _____ Phone #: _____

Address: _____ City: _____ State/Prov: _____ Zip/PC: _____

Creative Interventions for Troubled Children & Youth: US $25 CDN $30 QTY _____
More Creative Interventions for Troubled Children & Youth: US $25 CDN $30 QTY _____
Paper Dolls and Paper Airplanes: Therapeutic Exercises for Sexually Traumatized Children: US $40 CDN $60 QTY _____
Special offer: Buy all three books for $80.00 US or $105.00 CDN

Shipping: Orders under $40.00 add $5.00, orders over $40.00 add 15%. Canadians add 7% GST on total.
<u>All orders must be pre-paid.</u> Cash or cheque payable to Liana Lowenstein. Total enclosed:_____

Mail order form with payment to:
Liana Lowenstein, Pharma Plus, PO Box 91012, 2901 Bayview Avenue, Toronto, ON, M2K 1H0 Canada

For further information contact Liana Lowenstein: Tel: 416-575-7836 Email: liana@globalserve.net
Thank you for your order!

BIBLIOGRAPHY FOR PROFESSIONALS

Child Development

Davies, D. (1999). *Child development: A practitioner's guide.* New York: Guilford Press.

Mahler, M. (1975). *The psychological birth of the human infant.* New York: Basic Books.

Miller, A. (1981). *The drama of the gifted child: The search for the true self.* New York: Basic Books.

Neubauer, P. (ed.) (1976). *The process of child development.* New York: Meridian.

Piaget, J. (1970). *Piaget's theory. In P.H. Mussen (ed.), Carmichael's manual of child psychology.* New York: Wiley.

Pine, F. (1985). *Developmental theory and clinical process.* New Haven: Yale University Press.

Child Management

Barkley, R. (1987). *Defiant children: A clinician's manual for parent-training.* New York, NY: The Guilford Press.

Cline, V. (1980). *How to make your child a winner, 10 keys to rearing successful children.* Walker Publishing Co., Inc.

Coloroso, B. (1994). *Kids are worth it.* Toronto: Somerville House Publishing.

Dreikurs, R. (1972). *Coping with children's misbehavior.* New York: Hawthorn Press.

Gordon, T. (1970). *Parent effectiveness training.* New York: Wyden.

Psychopathology and Trauma

Anthony, E.J. and Cohler, B.J. (eds.) (1987). *The invulnerable child.* New York: The Guilford Press.

Bolby, J. (1982). *Attachment and loss (Vol.1): Attachment.* New York: Basic Books.

Bolby, J. (1983). *Attachment and loss (Vol.2): Separation (Rev. ed.).* New York: Basic Books.

Brandon, N. (1967). *The psychology of self-esteem.* New York: Bantam.

Brohl, K. (1996). *Working with traumatized children: A handbook for healing.* Washington, DC: CWLA Press.

Bynner, J.M., O'Malley, P.M., and Bachman, J.G. (1981). Self-esteem and delinquency revisited. *Journal of Youth and Adolescence,* 10, 407-441.

Carlson, E.B. (1997). *Trauma assessments: A clinician's guide.* New York: The Guilford Press.

Eth, S., and Pynoos, R. (eds.) (1985). *Post traumatic stress disorder in children.* Washington, D.C: American Psychiatric Press.

Hindman, J. (1989). *Just before dawn.* Ontario, Oregon: AlexAndria Associates.

James, B. (1994). *Handbook for treatment of attachment-trauma problems in children.* New York: The Free Press.

Johnson, K. (1989). *Trauma in the lives of children.* Claremount, CA: Hunter House.

Kernberg, P. and Chazan, S.E. (1991). *Children with conduct disorders: A psychotherapy manual.* New York: Basic Books.

Kordich-Hall, D. (1993). *Assessing child trauma.* Toronto: The Institute for the Prevention of Child Abuse.

Littner, N. (1960). The child's need to repeat his past: Some implications for placement. *Social Service Review,* 34, 128-148.

Monahon, C. (1993). *Children and trauma: A parent's guide to helping children heal.* New York, NY: Lexington Books.

Paul, H.A. (1995). *When kids are mad, not bad.* New York: Berkley Books.

Rubin, L. (1996). *The transcendent child: Tales of triumph over the past.* New York, NY: Basic Books.

Terr, L.C. (1990). *Too scared to cry: Psychic trauma in childhood.* New York: Harper and Row.

Van Der Kolk, B. A. (1987). *Psychological trauma.* Washington, DC: American Psychiatric Press.

Wolin, S. and Wolin, S. (1993). *The resilient self: How survivors of troubled families rise above adversity.* New York: Villard Books.

Play Therapy and Psychotherapy

Barnes, M. (1991). *"Endings."* Playground. Winter, p.8.

Burns, M. (1993). *Time in: A handbook for child and youth care professionals.* Canada: Burns-Johnston Publishing.

Crisci, G., Lay, M., and Lowenstein, L. (1997). *Paper dolls & paper airplanes: Therapeutic exercises for sexually traumatized children.* Charlotte, NC: Kidsrights Press.

Dodds, J.B. (1985). *A child psychotherapy primer: Suggestions for the beginning therapist.* New York: Human Sciences Press.

Duphouse, J.W. (1968). "Music Therapy: A valuable adjunct to psychotherapy with children." *Psychiatric Quarterly Supplement,* 42(1), p. 75-78.

Fox, E., Nelson, M. and Bolman, W. (1969). "The termination process: A neglected dimension in social work." *Social Work,* 14 (4), 53-63.

Gibson, R.L. (1993). *Counseling in the elementary school.* New York: Allyn & Bacon.

Gil, E. (1991). *The healing power of play.* New York: The Guilford Press.

Gondor, E.I. (1954). *Art and play therapy.* New York: Doubleday & Company Inc.

James, B. (1989). *Treating traumatized children.* Lexington, MA: Lexington Books.

James, O. (1997). *Play therapy: A comprehensive guide.* New Jersey: Jason Aronson Inc.

Kaduson, H.G., Cangelosi, D., and Schaefer, C.E. (eds.). (1997). *The playing cure: Individualized play therapy for specific childhood problems.* Northvale, NJ: Jason Aronson Inc.

Korman, S. and Stechler, G. (1985). *Making the jump to systems: The handbook of adolescent and family therapy.* New York: Gardner Press.

Lazarus, A. (1981). *The practice of multimodal therapy.* New York: McGraw-Hill.

Lockwood, J. (1973). "Psychodrama: A therapeutic tool with children in group play therapy." *Group Psychotherapy & Psychodrama,* 26(3-4), p.53-67.

Lowenstein, L. (1995). "The resolution scrapbook as an aid in the treatment of traumatized Children." *Child Welfare.* 74:4: 889-904.

Lowenstein, L. (2002). *More Creative Interventions for Troubled Children and Youth.* Toronto: Champion Press. (To order call: 416-575-7836)

Lubimiv, G.P. (1994). *Wings for our children: Essentials of becoming a play therapist.* Burnstown, ON: General Store Publishing House.

Moustakas Clark E. (1992). *Psychotherapy with children: The living relationship.* Greely, CO: Carron Publishers.

Naumberg, M. (1973). *An introduction to art therapy.* New York: Teachers College Press.

Oaklander, V. (1988). *Windows to our children.* Highland, NY: The Center for Gestalt Development.

Rubin, J. (1984). *Child art therapy.* New York: Van Nostrand Reinhold Company.

Schaefer, C. E. (1981). *The therapeutic use of child's play.* New York: Jason Aronson.

Schaefer, C.E. and O'Connor, K.J. (eds.) (1983). *Handbook of play therapy.* New York: John Wiley & Sons.

Schaefer, C. E. and Reid, S.E. (eds.) (1986). *Game play: Therapeutic use of childhood games.* New York: John Wiley and sons.

Stern, J.B. and Fodor, I.G. (1989). "Anger control in children: A review of social skills and cognitive behavioral approaches to deal with aggressive children." *Child and Family Behavior Therapy,* 11, 1-20.

Group psychotherapy

Corder, B.F. (1994). *Structured adolescent psychotherapy groups.* Sarasota, FL: Professional Resource Press.

Corey, G., Corey, M. S. (1977). *Groups: Process and practice.* Monterey, CA: Brooks-Cole.

Lennox, D. (1982). *Residential group therapy for children.* London: Tavistock Publications.

Northen, H. (1988). *Social work with groups.* New York: Columbia University Press.

Rose, S., and Edleson, J. (1987). *Working with children and adolescents in groups.* San Francisco: Jossey-Bass Publishers.

Yalom, I. (1975). *The theory and practice of group psychotherapy.* New York: Basic Books.

BIBLIOGRAPHY FOR CHILDREN

Feelings

Bennett Blackburn, L. (1991). *I know I made it happen.* Centering Corporation, Box 3367, Omaha, NE 68103. 402-553-1200. (Ages 6-12)

Best, A. (1989). *That makes me angry!* Racine, WI: Golden Books. (Ages 4-8)

Hazen, B. (1992). *Even if I did something awful.* Toronto: Maxwell MacMillan, Canada. (Ages 6-12)

Herzfeld, G., and Powell, R. (1986). *Coping for kids.* West Nyack, NY: The Center for Applied Research in Education. Order from Prentice Hall, Prentice Hall Bldg., Englewood Cliffs, NJ 07632. Phone: 201-767-5030. (Ages 8 and up)

Social Skills

Berenstein, S., and Berenstein, J. (1982). *The berenstein bears get in a fight.* New York: Random House. (Ages 4-8)

Booth, Z. (1987). *Finding a friend.* Mount Desert, ME: Windswept. (Ages 4-10)

Goffe, T. (1991). *Bully for you.* New York: Child's Play. (Ages 8-12)

Powell, R. (1990). *How to deal with friends.* Mahwah, NJ: Troll. (Ages 4-8)

Scott, S. (1986). *How to say no and keep your friends.* Amherst, MA: Human Resource Development Press Inc. (Ages 10 and up)

Terrell, R.(1992). *A kid's guide to how to stop violence.* New York: Avon. (Ages 10 and up)

Self-esteem

Bannatyne-Cugnet, J. (1993). *Estelle and the self-esteem machine.* Red Deer Alberta: Red Deer College Press. (Ages 6-12)

Johnson, J. (1991). *Celebrate you: Building your self-esteem.* Minneapolis: Lerner. (Ages 10 and up)

Loomans, D. *The lovables in the kingdom of self-esteem.* Tiburon, CA: H.J. Kramer, Inc. (Ages 4-10)

Palmer, P. (1989). *Teen esteem.* San Luis Obispo, CA: Impact Press (Ages 12 and up)

RESOURCES

Candy stores

Chocolate gold coins, DWEEBS®, NERDS®, RUNTS®.

Craft and office supply stores

Adhesive dots, banner paper, brass pot, card stock, clay, colored paper, coloring supplies, envelopes, flip chart paper, glitter, glue sticks, index cards, journals, pom poms, poster board, scissors, stickers, tape, tissue paper.

Game supply stores

Dice, poker chips.

Party supply stores

Party decorations, balloons, gift bags, invitations, loot bags, party hats, party horns, Pin the Tail on the Donkey game.

Toy stores and novelty shops

BLOPENS®, bubbles, building blocks, dart games, dice, friendship bracelets, paints, Pin the Tail on the Donkey game, plastic tea set, puzzles, rubber stamp kits, stickers, stress balls, stuffed animals, tattoos, The CANDY LAND® game, The HOT POTATO game, NERF® basketball, the PERFECTION ® game, the TROUBLE® game, YAK BAK®.

Miscellaneous items

BLOPENS ® and mouthpieces available by calling 1-888-517-7180. Request set of 10 BLOPENS ® for $9.99 and additional mouthpieces.

The Electronic Talking HOT POTATO ® can be purchased on the Internet from TOYSMART.COM item # HB40385.

YAK BAK ® micro-recorders are available in most retail outlets. For more information, call: 1-800-222-9376.

Inexpensive prizes, friendship bracelets, happy face novelty items, stickers, stress balls, available through Smilemakers mail order catalogue, Station St., Unit 4, Ajax, Ontario. L1S 3HZ. 905-686-3663. In Canada: 800-667-5000. In the United States: 800-825-8085.

ABOUT THE AUTHOR

Liana Lowenstein, M.S.W., RSW, CPT-S is a Registered Social Worker and Certified Play Therapist Supervisor. She maintains a private practice in Toronto, Canada, where she specializes in assessment and treatment services for children with a variety of emotional difficulties. In addition to her clinical work, Liana lectures internationally on topics related to child trauma and play therapy, and she provides clinical supervision and consultation to therapists and mental health agencies.

Liana has authored numerous publications including the books, *Paper Dolls & Paper Airplanes: Therapeutic Exercises for Sexually Traumatized Children* (Crisci, Lay & Lowenstein, Kidsrights Press, 1997) and *More Creative Interventions for Troubled Children & Youth* (Champion Press, 2002).